Brooklyn Tweed's CAPSULE *series is an opportunity for a single independent designer to explore a source of inspiration and produce a focused collection using BT yarns.*

CAPSULE

Winter 2017

MICHELE WANG

CONTENTS

43
PATTERNS

129
GLOSSARY

136
INFO

LETTER

FROM MICHELE

This Capsule has been a long time in the making, and the pieces in this collection are a summation of what a handknit means to me. More than any other type of clothing, knits are like old friends. I often wrap a handknit around me as I get ready to lounge on the couch, stay in for the evening with a good book, or knit in my favorite chair — whether or not I need the extra warmth. It's more a matter of wrapping up for comfort of mind.

Since I first laid hands on Shelter, and later Loft and Quarry, the unique tactile qualities of the Targhee-Columbia fleece and the cloudlike structure of woolen-spun yarn have evoked images of my favorite kind of cozy home living. The lightweight fabric these yarns produce calls out to be used for layering pieces — garments that give you that cuddle-down comfort even when you have to venture out and face the world.

ASPEN is my idea of the quintessential loungewear centerpiece: the knitted robe. I designed a coordinated men's piece, RADMERE, and indulged my love of cables yet again in the open-front ILIA and the grandpa-style CELYN cardigan. And for those days when you need clean and simple, PALMER is the perfect staple companion.

While I find cardigans to be the practical workhorses of my wardrobe, there's no substitute for a pullover if you want something substantial, warm and enveloping. BINGHAM and HAGUE each incorporate elements I love in relaxed pieces: the shawl collar, which keeps the chill from your neck, and the drop shoulder, for a shape you can comfortably throw on over a T-shirt. I finished the collection with CLERIDAE, a cabled cap with a pompom.

All of the designs in the collection were made with you, the knitter, in mind. I hope I've been able to create pieces that will become your old friends.

COLLECTION

|

9

ILIA

CARDIGAN

Add structural flair to your wardrobe with a plush cabled cardigan. Wide bands of front ribbing fold back to form a collar and create an architectural silhouette. The densely worked fabric features rope cables spliced into a lattice for vivid texture and cozy warmth. The double-ribbed hem extends into ribbed side panels that punctuate the cabled motif for visual balance. Ilia's boxy fit makes for easy layering; the fronts may be pinned to close if you wish, so choose a size that gives you 3-5" of ease with the fronts overlapped.

HAGUE

PULLOVER

|

Corrugated texture provides a trellis for twining cables at the center front and back. Hague sports a boxy silhouette with a bateau neck and exaggerated drop shoulders that create a chevron detail where the welts meet at the seam line. This pullover is a quick knit in chunky Quarry, and the bold texture of this garment means the motifs won't be lost in our darker colors. The sample is shown in Slate, but Lazulite and even Obsidian would be handsome choices, too.

RADMERE

CARDIGAN

This luxuriously cabled cardigan updates a classic
masculine style with a modern slimmer fit in the sleeves.
Radmere's trimly tailored shoulders are crowned with an
extra-large shawl collar, and the densely cabled fabric
in Shelter makes it warm enough to wear as a jacket in
soft autumn weather. The intricate stitchwork will show
to best advantage in light or bright colors; imagine it
in a striking red like Long Johns or a mellow grey like
Sweatshirt for very different effects.

PALMER

CARDIGAN

For simple, elegant style, reach for a long, open-front cardigan. Palmer's light fabric of Loft makes it warm but weightless, and its minimalist design highlights a few perfect details like fully fashioned shoulders and generous pockets. The deep single-rib hem draws in to gently shape the otherwise straight silhouette. Palmer is a versatile garment that will suit almost any occasion, so choose a color that will complement everything in your closet.

BINGHAM

PULLOVER

When your lounging agenda demands serious hygge, it's hard to beat a shawl-collared pullover in chunky wool. Bingham works up rapidly in Quarry, with the hem knit in a variable rib that sets up engaging panels of cables feeding into a central plait on the front and back. A straight torso and raglan shoulder shaping create a relaxed look without sacrificing good design; the decrease rate shifts subtly to nibble away excess fabric for an anatomical fit.

CELYN

CARDIGAN

Slantwise texture distinguishes this timeless V-neck cardigan. A directional lattice of cabled ribs is mirrored on the fronts, but slants across the full width of the back to create unexpected asymmetrical movement. Celyn's stockinette sleeves are set in, with fully fashioned decreases to elegantly shape the caps. The elongated silhouette is shaped with a gentle A-line for a comfortable, flattering fit. As handsome over button-downs as it is cozy over pajamas on a lazy Sunday, this versatile cardigan in Shelter has wardrobe staple written all over it.

CLERIDAE

HAT

|

For casual weekend errands, throw on this organically cabled hat that recalls patches of sky glimpsed from the forest floor. Sturdy cabled trunks interspersed among the ribs of the brim branch into more delicate interlacing motifs on a ground of reverse stockinette. The ribbed crown finishes with a jaunty pompom, if you so desire. Try it in your favorite bright accent color from the Shelter palette or choose a wear-with-everything neutral like Fossil or Snowbound.

ASPEN

ROBE CARDIGAN

|

Wonderfully warm on winter mornings as it may be, this knee-length knitted robe in Shelter is too beautiful to confine to the house. A symphony of extravagant cables demands public appreciation. On top of its ornate motifs, Aspen boasts a full array of perfect details: a large shawl collar shaped with short rows, set-in sleeves, generous pockets, a ribbed belt and belt loops. Subtle A-line shaping allows for easy movement within a trim silhouette. This robe is a master class in cable knitting; choose a light-colored yarn to best display your work.

PATTERNS

43

ILIA

OVERVIEW

SCHEMATIC
46

PATTERN
47

CHARTS
53

MATERIALS

2985 (3235, 3730, 3960, 4420, 4710) yards of fingering weight wool yarn
11 (12, 14, 15, 17, 18) skeins Brooklyn Tweed *Loft* (100% American Targhee-Columbia Wool; 275 yards/50 grams)

Photographed in color *Sweatshirt*

GAUGE

38 stitches & 40 rows = 4" in chart patterns with Size A needle(s), after blocking
One 32-stitch & 30-row repeat from any chart measures approximately 3¼" wide and 3" tall with Size A needle(s), after blocking

NEEDLES

Size A (for Main Fabric)
One 32" circular needle in size needed to obtain gauge listed
Suggested Size: 3½ mm (US 4)
Size B (for Ribbing)
One 40" circular needle, one size smaller than Size A
Suggested Size: 3¼ mm (US 3)

Focused energy. An orderly cable pattern hums with synchronized action. A showy, open-front silhouette lets your knitting stand proud.

ADDITIONAL TOOLS

Stitch markers, removable markers, cable needle (CN), T-pins (optional), blunt tapestry needle, a small amount of sock yarn in a similar color for seaming (see *Construction Notes*)

FINISHED DIMENSIONS

35½ (39¼, 43, 46¼, 49¼, 52½)" [90 (99.5, 109, 117.5, 125, 133.5) cm] circumference at bust, with collar overlapped
Intended Ease: + 3–5" [7.5–12.5 cm]
Sample shown is size 39¼" [99.5 cm] with 5¼" [13.5 cm] ease on model

SKILL LEVEL

● ● ● ● ○

CONSTRUCTION NOTES

The cardigan is worked in pieces from the bottom up and then sewn together. The collar is picked up around the front edges and back neck edge and worked flat.

The Sloped Bind Off (see *Special Techniques*) is used when shaping the armholes, shoulders, and sleeve caps.

Read RS (odd-numbered) chart rows from right to left; read WS (even-numbered) chart rows from left to right. Review the charts carefully as a different chart is used for each piece.

The chart includes left and right cable crosses (LC and RC) where knit stitches are crossed over knit stitches and left and right cable twists (LT and RT) where knit stitches are crossed over purl stitches.

While working shaping or when a start/end point for your size intersects a cable, if you do not have enough stitches to complete the cable, work the affected stitches as knit or purl as they appear.

Where {knit 1} appears in braces, it indicates a selvedge stitch.

Pieces are worked flat on a circular needle to accommodate the large number of stitches. A longer Size B needle is required due to the width of the collar.

Because of the softly spun nature of *Loft*, some knitters prefer to do their seaming with a firmly spun yarn, such as sock yarn, in a similar color; alternatively, you may add twist into the yarn (in the same direction as the yarn is plied) as you seam to add tensile strength.

ILIA

SCHEMATIC

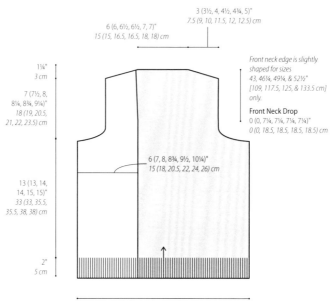

3 (3½, 4, 4½, 4¾, 5)"
7.5 (9, 10, 11.5, 12, 12.5) cm

6 (6, 6½, 6½, 7, 7)"
15 (15, 16.5, 16.5, 18, 18) cm

1¼"
3 cm

7 (7½, 8,
8¼, 8¾, 9¼)"
18 (19, 20.5,
21, 22, 23.5) cm

*Front neck edge is slightly
shaped for sizes
43, 46¼, 49¼, & 52½"
[109, 117.5, 125, & 133.5 cm]
only.*

Front Neck Drop
0 (0, 7¼, 7¼, 7¼, 7¼)"
0 (0, 18.5, 18.5, 18.5, 18.5) cm

6 (7, 8, 8¾, 9½, 10¼)"
15 (18, 20.5, 22, 24, 26) cm

13 (13, 14,
14, 15, 15)"
33 (33, 35.5,
35.5, 38, 38) cm

2"
5 cm

18 (19¾, 21½, 23¼, 24¾, 26½)"
45.5 (50, 54.5, 59, 63, 67.5) cm

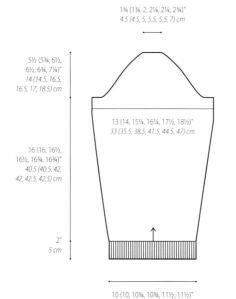

1¾ (1¾, 2, 2¼, 2¼, 2¾)"
4.5 (4.5, 5, 5.5, 5.5, 7) cm

5½ (5¾, 6½,
6½, 6¾, 7¼)"
14 (14.5, 16.5,
16.5, 17, 18.5) cm

13 (14, 15¼, 16¼, 17½, 18½)"
33 (35.5, 38.5, 41.5, 44.5, 47) cm

16 (16, 16½,
16½, 16¾, 16¾)"
40.5 (40.5, 42,
42, 42.5, 42.5) cm

2"
5 cm

10 (10, 10¾, 10¾, 11½, 11½)"
25.5 (25.5, 27.5, 27.5, 29, 29) cm

ILIA

STITCH PATTERN

2X2 RIBBING
Multiple of 4 stitches; 2-row repeat

Row 1 (RS): {Knit 1}, knit 2, *purl 2, knit 2; repeat from * to last stitch, {knit 1}.
Row 2 (WS): {Knit 1}, purl 2, *knit 2, purl 2; repeat from * to last stitch, {knit 1}.

Repeat Rows 1 & 2 for pattern.

BACK

With Size B 40" circular needle (suggested size: 3¼ mm/US 3) cast on 172 (188, 204, 220, 236, 252) stitches using your preferred method. Do not join; work back and forth in rows.

WORK RIBBING
Begin 2x2 Ribbing (see *Stitch Pattern*); work even until piece measures approximately 2" from cast-on edge, ending with a WS row.

BEGIN MAIN PATTERN
Switch to Size A 32" circular needle (suggested size: 3½ mm/US 4).

Next Row (RS): {Knit 1}, beginning and ending where indicated for your size, work Row 1 of Chart A to last stitch, working 32-stitch repeat 5 (5, 6, 6, 7, 7) times, {knit 1}.

Next Row (WS): {Knit 1}, work Row 2 of Chart A to last stitch, {knit 1}.

Work even in established pattern until piece measures 15 (15, 16, 16, 17, 17)" from cast-on edge, ending with a WS row.

SHAPE ARMHOLES
Please review Sloped Bind Off and Binding Off Over Cabled Fabrics (see Special Techniques) before proceeding. Bind off in pattern.

Bind off 12 (15, 16, 18, 19, 20) stitches at the beginning of the next 2 rows, then bind off 8 stitches at the beginning of the next 2 rows, then bind off 4 stitches at the beginning of the next 2 rows, then bind off 2 stitches at the beginning of the next 2 rows, then bind off 1 stitch at the beginning of the next 4 (6, 6, 10, 16, 22) rows. [116 (124, 138, 146, 154, 162) stitches remain]

Next Row (RS): {Knit 1}, work as established to last stitch, {knit 1}.

Work even as established until armholes measure 7 (7½, 8, 8¼, 8¾, 9¼)", ending with a WS row.

SHAPE SHOULDERS
Use the Sloped Bind Off and work according to Binding Off Over Cabled Fabrics for best results. Bind off in pattern.

Bind off 5 (5, 6, 7, 7, 8) stitches at the beginning of the next 6 rows, then bind off 5 (6, 7, 7, 8, 8) stitches at the beginning of the next 4 rows, then bind off 4 (6, 6, 7, 7, 8) stitches at the beginning of the next 2 rows. [58 (58, 62, 62, 66, 66) stitches remain]

Bind off remaining stitches.

LEFT FRONT

With Size B 40" circular needle cast on 58 (66, 74, 82, 90, 98) using your preferred method.

WORK RIBBING
Row 1 (RS): {Knit 1}, *knit 2, purl 2; repeat from * to last stitch, {knit 1}.
Row 2 (WS): Repeat Row 1.

Repeat the last 2 rows until piece measures 2" from cast-on edge, ending with a WS (WS, RS, RS, WS, WS) row.

Sizes 43 & 46¼" Only:
Increase Row (WS): {Knit 1}, M1P, work in established rib to last stitch, {knit 1}. [– (–, 75, 83, –, –) stitches now on needle]

All Sizes Resume:
BEGIN MAIN PATTERN
Switch to Size A 32" circular needle.

Next Row (RS): {Knit 1}, beginning and ending where indicated for your size, work Row 1 of Chart B to last stitch, working 32-stitch repeat 1 (1, 2, 2, 2, 2) time(s), {knit 1}.

Next Row (WS): {Knit 1}, work Row 2 of Chart B to last stitch, {knit 1}.

Work even in established pattern until piece measures 15 (15, 16, 16, 17, 17)" from cast-on edge, ending with a WS row.

SHAPE ARMHOLE
Use the Sloped Bind Off and work according to Binding Off Over Cabled Fabrics for best results. Bind off in pattern. When armhole shaping is complete, continue in chart pattern over remaining stitches.

Bind off 12 (15, 16, 18, 19, 20) stitches at the beginning of the next RS row, then bind off 8 stitches at the beginning of the following RS row, then bind off 4 stitches at the beginning of the next RS row, then bind off 2 stitches at the beginning of the next RS row, then bind off 1 stitch at the beginning of the next 2 (3, 3, 5, 8, 11) RS rows. [30 (34, 42, 46, 49, 53) stitches remain]

Next Row (WS): {Knit 1}, work as established to last stitch, {knit 1}.

Sizes 43, 46¼, 49¼, & 52½" Only:

Work even in established pattern until armhole measures – (–, 2, 2¼, 2¾, 3¼)", ending with a WS row.

Front Edge Decrease Row (RS): Work as established to last 3 stitches, SSP (or SSK to keep in pattern), {knit 1}. (1 stitch decreased)

Repeat the Front Edge Decrease Row every – (–, 24th, 24th, 16th, 16th) row – (–, 2, 2, 3, 3) more times.

Upon completion of this section, you will have worked the Front Edge Decrease Row a total of – (–, 3, 3, 4, 4) times; you now have – (–, 39, 43, 45, 49) stitches on your needle.

All Sizes Resume:

Work even in established pattern until armhole measures 7 (7½, 8, 8¼, 8¾, 9¼)", ending with a WS row.

SHAPE SHOULDERS

Use the Sloped Bind Off and work according to Binding Off Over Cabled Fabrics for best results. Bind off in pattern.

Bind off 5 (5, 6, 7, 7, 8) stitches at the beginning of the next 3 RS rows, then bind off 5 (6, 7, 7, 8, 8) stitches at the beginning of the following 2 RS rows. [5 (7, 7, 8, 8, 9) stitches remain]

Bind off remaining stitches on next RS row.

RIGHT FRONT

With Size B 40" circular needle cast on 58 (66, 74, 82, 90, 98) stitches using your preferred method.

WORK RIBBING

Row 1 (RS): {Knit 1}, *purl 2, knit 2; repeat from * to last stitch, {knit 1}.

Row 2 (WS): Repeat Row 1.

Repeat the last 2 rows until piece measures 2" from cast-on edge, ending with a WS (WS, RS, RS, WS, WS) row.

Sizes 43 & 46¼" Only:

Increase Row (WS): {Knit 1}, work in established rib to last stitch, M1P, {knit 1}. [– (–, 75, 83, –, –) stitches now on needle]

All Sizes Resume:

BEGIN MAIN PATTERN

Switch to Size A 32" circular needle.

Next Row (RS): {Knit 1}, beginning and ending where indicated for your size, work Row 1 of Chart C to last stitch, working 32-stitch repeat 1 (1, 2, 2, 2, 2) time(s), {knit 1}.

Next Row (WS): {Knit 1}, work Row 2 of Chart C to last stitch, {knit 1}.

Work even in established pattern until piece measures 15 (15, 16, 16, 17, 17)" from cast-on edge, ending with a RS row.

SHAPE ARMHOLE

Use the Sloped Bind Off and work according to Binding Off Over Cabled Fabrics for best results. Bind off in pattern. When armhole shaping is complete, continue in chart pattern over remaining stitches.

Bind off 12 (15, 16, 18, 19, 20) stitches at the beginning of the next WS row, then bind off 8 stitches at the beginning of the following WS row, then bind off 4 stitches at the beginning of the next WS row, then bind off 2 stitches at the beginning of the next WS row, then bind off 1 stitch at the beginning of the next 2 (3, 3, 5, 8, 11) WS rows. [30 (34, 42, 46, 49, 53) stitches remain]

Next Row (RS): {Knit 1}, work as established to last stitch, {knit 1}.

Sizes 43, 46¼, 49¼, & 52½" Only:
Work even in established pattern until armhole measures – (–, 2, 2¼, 2¾, 3¼)", ending with a WS row.

Front Edge Decrease Row (RS): {Knit 1}, p2tog (or k2tog to keep in pattern), work as established to end. (1 stitch decreased)

Repeat the Front Edge Decrease Row every – (–, 24th, 24th, 16th, 16th) row – (–, 2, 2, 3, 3) more times.

Upon completion of this section, you will have worked the Front Edge Decrease Row a total of – (–, 3, 3, 4, 4) times; you now have – (–, 39, 43, 45, 49) stitches on your needle.

All Sizes Resume:
Work even in established pattern until armhole measures 7 (7½, 8, 8¼, 8¾, 9¼)", ending with a RS row.

SHAPE SHOULDERS

Use the Sloped Bind Off and work according to Binding Off Over Cabled Fabrics for best results. Bind off in pattern.

Bind off 5 (5, 6, 7, 7, 8) stitches at the beginning of the next 3 WS rows, then bind off 5 (6, 7, 7, 8, 8) stitches at the beginning of the following 2 WS rows. [5 (7, 7, 8, 8, 9) stitches remain]

Bind off remaining stitches on next WS row.

LEFT SLEEVE

With Size B 40" circular needle cast on 94 (94, 102, 102, 110, 110) stitches using your preferred method.

WORK RIBBING

Row 1 (RS): {Knit 1}, *knit 2, purl 2; repeat from * to last stitch, {knit 1}.
Row 2 (WS): Repeat Row 1.

Repeat the last 2 rows until piece measures 2" from cast-on edge, ending with a WS row.

BEGIN MAIN PATTERN

Switch to Size A 32" circular needle.

Next Row (RS): {Knit 1}, beginning and ending where indicated for your size, work Row 1 of Chart D to last stitch, working 32-stitch repeat twice, {knit 1}.

Next Row (WS): {Knit 1}, work Row 2 of Chart D to last stitch, {knit 1}.

Work even in established pattern for 6 more rows, ending with a WS row.

SHAPE SLEEVE

Sleeve Increase Row (RS): {Knit 1}, M1R (or M1P to keep in pattern), work as established to last stitch, M1L (or M1P to keep in pattern), {knit 1}. (2 stitches increased)

Repeat the Sleeve Increase Row every 10th (8th, 8th, 6th, 6th, 6th) row 12 (11, 11, 21, 18, 8) more times, then every 8th (6th, 6th, 4th, 4th, 4th) row 2 (8, 9, 4, 9, 24) times, working new stitches into pattern.

Upon completion of this section, you will have worked the Sleeve Increase Row a total of 15 (20, 21, 26, 28, 33) times; you now have 124 (134, 144, 154, 166, 176) stitches on your needle.

Work even in established pattern until piece measures 18 (18, 18½, 18½, 18¾, 18¾)" from cast-on edge, ending with a WS row.

SHAPE SLEEVE CAP

Use the Sloped Bind Off and work according to Binding Off Over Cabled Fabrics for best results. Bind off in pattern.

Bind off 12 (15, 16, 18, 19, 20) stitches at the beginning of the next 2 rows, then bind off 8 stitches at the beginning of the following 2 rows, then bind off 2 stitches at the beginning of the next 2 (2, 2, 2, 4, 4) rows. [80 (84, 92, 98, 104, 112) stitches remain]

Cap Decrease Row (RS): {Knit 1}, k2tog (or p2tog to keep in pattern), work as established to last 3 stitches, SSK (or SSP to keep in pattern), {knit 1}. (2 stitches decreased)

Repeat the Cap Decrease Row every RS row 21 (23, 26, 27, 26, 28) more times. [36 (36, 38, 42, 50, 54) stitches remain]

Work 1 row even (WS).

Bind off 4 stitches at the beginning of the next 2 (2, 2, 2, 4, 4) rows, then bind off 6 stitches at the beginning of the following 2 rows. [16 (16, 18, 22, 22, 26) stitches remain]

Bind off remaining stitches, working according to Binding Off Over Cabled Fabrics.

RIGHT SLEEVE

Work as for left sleeve, working Chart E instead of Chart D.

FINISHING

Wet-block pieces to schematic measurements (see *Special Techniques*). With matching sock yarn threaded on a tapestry needle, sew shoulder seams (see *Construction Notes*).

COLLAR

With Size B 40" circular needle, RS facing, and beginning at bottom of right front, pick up and knit 148 (150, 164, 166, 176, 178) stitches up right front edge to shoulder seam, 50 (50, 54, 54, 58, 58) stitches evenly along back neck, and 148 (150, 164, 166, 176, 178) stitches down left front edge, ending at bottom edge. [346 (350, 382, 386, 410, 414) stitches now on needle]

Next Row (WS): Slip 1 purlwise wyif, purl 1, *knit 2, purl 2; repeat from * to end.
Next Row (RS): Slip 1 purlwise wyib, knit 1, *purl 2, knit 2; repeat from * to end.

Work even in established rib until collar measures 6".

Bind off all stitches in pattern.

Sew side and sleeve seams. Set in sleeves, taking care to place left and right sleeves correctly. Fold collar back 3". Steam collar and seams gently or wet-block entire garment again.

CHART A: BACK

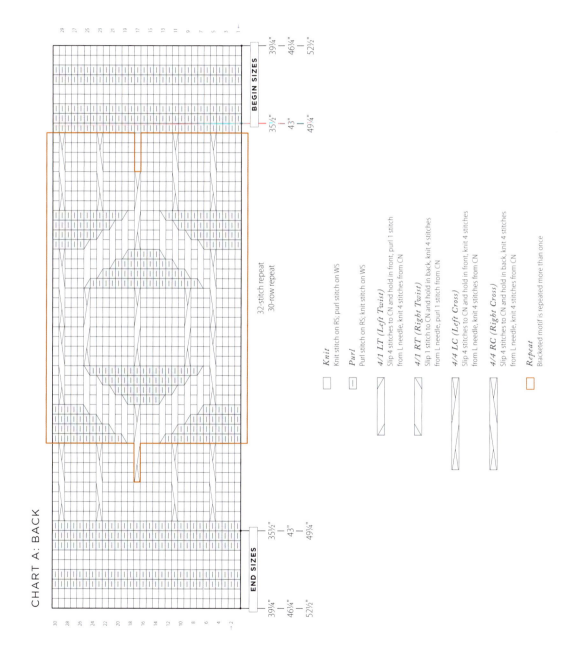

Knit
Knit stitch on RS, purl stitch on WS

Purl
Purl stitch on RS, knit stitch on WS

4/1 LT (Left Twist)
Slip 4 stitches to CN and hold in front, purl 1 stitch from L needle, knit 4 stitches from CN

4/1 RT (Right Twist)
Slip 1 stitch to CN and hold in back, knit 4 stitches from L needle, purl 1 stitch from CN

4/4 LC (Left Cross)
Slip 4 stitches to CN and hold in front, knit 4 stitches from L needle, knit 4 stitches from CN

4/4 RC (Right Cross)
Slip 4 stitches to CN and hold in back, knit 4 stitches from L needle, knit 4 stitches from CN

Repeat
Bracketed motif is repeated more than once

32-stitch repeat
30-row repeat

BEGIN SIZES

39¼"
46¼"
52½"

35½"
43"
49¼"

END SIZES

35½"
43"
49¼"

39¼"
46¼"
52½"

ILIA

CHARTS

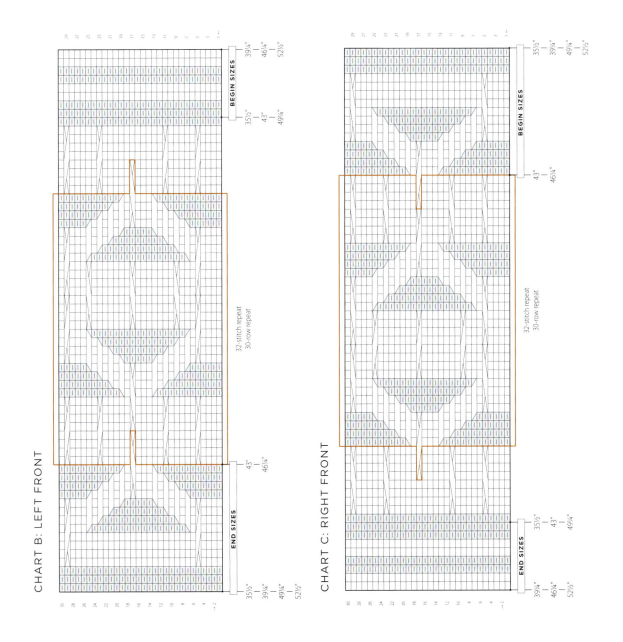

CHART B: LEFT FRONT

CHART C: RIGHT FRONT

54

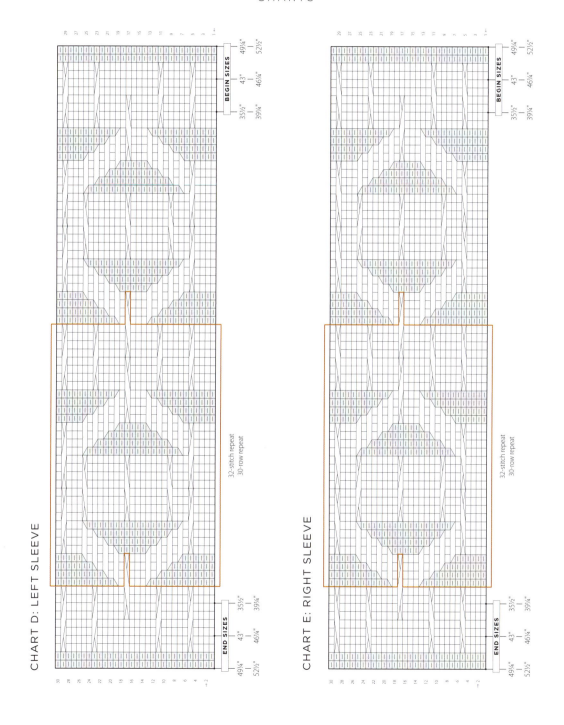

CHART D: LEFT SLEEVE

CHART E: RIGHT SLEEVE

32-stitch repeat
30-row repeat

BEGIN SIZES

49¼"
52½"

43"
46¼"

35½"
39¼"

END SIZES

35½"
39¼"

43"
46¼"

49¼"
52½"

HAGUE

OVERVIEW

SCHEMATIC
58

PATTERN
59

CHART
64

MATERIALS

1220 (1335, 1480, 1625, 1795, 1910) yards of chunky weight wool yarn

7 (7, 8, 9, 9, 10) skeins of Brooklyn Tweed *Quarry* (100% American Targhee-Columbia wool; 200 yards/100 grams)

Photographed in color *Slate*

GAUGE

13 stitches & 22 rows = 4" in Welt Pattern with Size A needle(s), after blocking

18 stitches & 22 rows = 4" in Chart Pattern with Size A needle(s), after blocking

NEEDLES

Size A (for Main Fabric)

One pair of straight needles or a 24" circular needle* in size needed to obtain gauge listed

Suggested Size: 8 mm (US 11)

Size B (for Ribbing)

One pair of straight needles or a 24" circular needle* and one 16" circular needle, two sizes smaller than Size A

Suggested Size: 6 mm (US 10)

Knitter's preferred style of needle may be used

Industrial geometry overgrown with twining vines. The boxy shape of this chunky, welted pullover is softened and grounded by pliant, spacious cables.

ADDITIONAL TOOLS

Stitch markers, locking markers or coilless safety pins, stitch holders or waste yarn, T-pins (optional), blunt tapestry needle, a small amount of a firmly spun worsted weight yarn in a similar color for seaming (see *Construction Notes*)

FINISHED DIMENSIONS

37¼ (40¾, 44¼, 48¼, 51¾, 55¾)" [94.5 (103.5, 112.5, 122.5, 131.5, 141.5) cm] circumference at bust
Intended Ease: + 4–6" [10–15 cm]
Sample shown is size 40¾" [103.5 cm] with 6¾" [17 cm] ease on model

SKILL LEVEL

● ● ● ○ ○

CONSTRUCTION NOTES

The pieces are worked flat from the bottom up and sewn together. The collar is picked up and worked circularly after garment assembly.

The Sloped Bind Off (see *Special Techniques*) is used at the shoulder and neck edges.

Read RS (odd-numbered) chart rows from right to left; read WS (even-numbered) chart rows from left to right.

The chart includes left and right cable crosses (LC and RC) where knit stitches are crossed over knit stitches and left and right cable twists (LT and RT) where knit stitches are crossed over purl stitches.

Where {knit 1} appears in braces, it indicates a selvedge stitch.

Because of the softly spun nature of *Quarry*, some knitters prefer to do their seaming with a firmly spun yarn in a similar color; alternatively, you may add twist into the yarn (in the same direction as the yarn is plied) as you seam to add tensile strength. When weaving in ends, twist the yarn several times in the same direction in which it is plied before threading the tapestry needle with the yarn end. Add more twist as you sew, if necessary. You may wish to weave in the ends as you go.

For more information on working with *Quarry*, see our Tip Card at www.brooklyntweed.com/tips/quarry.

HAGUE

SCHEMATIC

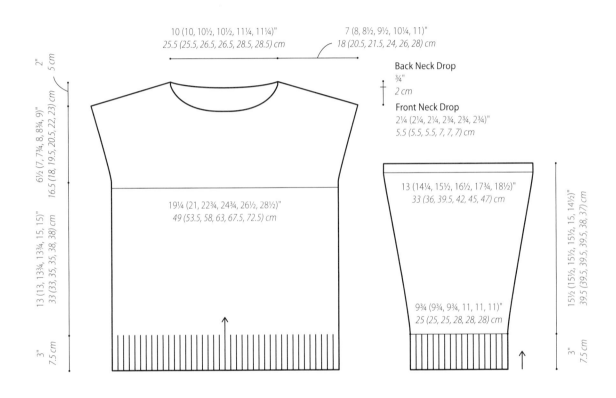

10 (10, 10½, 10½, 11¼, 11¼)"
25.5 (25.5, 26.5, 26.5, 28.5, 28.5) cm

7 (8, 8½, 9½, 10¼, 11)"
18 (20.5, 21.5, 24, 26, 28) cm

Back Neck Drop
¾"
2 cm

Front Neck Drop
2¼ (2¼, 2¼, 2¾, 2¾, 2¾)"
5.5 (5.5, 5.5, 7, 7, 7) cm

2"
5 cm

6½ (7, 7¾, 8, 8¾, 9)"
16.5 (18, 19.5, 20.5, 22, 23) cm

19¼ (21, 22¾, 24¾, 26½, 28½)"
49 (53.5, 58, 63, 67.5, 72.5) cm

13 (13, 13¾, 13¾, 15, 15)"
33 (33, 35, 35, 38, 38) cm

3"
7.5 cm

13 (14¼, 15½, 16½, 17¾, 18½)"
33 (36, 39.5, 42, 45, 47) cm

15½ (15½, 15½, 15½, 15, 14½)"
39.5 (39.5, 39.5, 39.5, 38, 37) cm

9¾ (9¾, 9¾, 11, 11, 11)"
25 (25, 25, 28, 28, 28) cm

3"
7.5 cm

HAGUE

STITCH PATTERNS

2X2 RIBBING
Multiple of 4 stitches; 2-row repeat

Row 1 (RS): {Knit 1}, knit 2, *purl 2, knit 2; repeat from * to last stitch, {knit 1}.
Row 2 (WS): {Knit 1}, purl 2, *knit 2, purl 2; repeat from * to last stitch, {knit 1}.

Repeat Rows 1 & 2 for pattern.

WELT PATTERN
Any number of stitches; 4-row repeat

Row 1 (RS): Purl.
Row 2 (WS): Knit.
Row 3: Knit.
Row 4: Purl.

Repeat Rows 1–4 for pattern.

BACK

With Size B needle(s) (suggested size: 6 mm/US 10) cast on 72 (80, 84, 92, 96, 104) stitches using your preferred method. Do not join; work back and forth in rows.

WORK RIBBING
Begin 2x2 Ribbing (see *Stitch Patterns*); work even until piece measures approximately 3" from cast-on edge, ending with a RS (WS, RS, WS, RS, WS) row.

Sizes 37¼, 44¼, & 51¾" Only:
Increase Row (WS): {Knit 1}, purl 2, M1L, work in established rib to last 3 stitches, M1R, purl 2, {knit 1}. [74 (–, 86, –, 98, –) stitches now on needle]

All Sizes Resume:
BEGIN MAIN PATTERN
Switch to Size A needle(s) (suggested size: 8 mm/US 11).

Next Row (RS): {Knit 1}, work Row 1 of Welt Pattern (see *Stitch Patterns*) over 15 (18, 21, 24, 27, 30) stitches, place marker, work Row 1 of Cable Chart over 42 stitches, place marker, work Row 1 of Welt Pattern to last stitch, {knit 1}.

Next Row (WS): {Knit 1}, work Row 2 of Welt Pattern to marker, slip marker, work Row 2 of Cable Chart to marker, slip marker, work Row 2 of Welt Pattern to last stitch, {knit 1}.

Work even in established pattern until piece measures 16 (16, 16¾, 16¾, 18, 18)" from cast-on edge, ending with a WS row.

SHAPE ARMHOLE EDGES

Place a locking marker or coilless safety pin in each side of the last row worked. This marks the beginning of the armhole section and will be used as a point of reference.

Work 4 (6, 6, 6, 6, 6) rows even in established pattern.

Armhole Edge Increase Row (RS): {Knit 1}, work 2 stitches in pattern, M1R (or M1P to keep in pattern), work as established to last 3 stitches, M1L (or M1P to keep in pattern), work 2 stitches in pattern, {knit 1}. (2 stitches increased)

Repeat the Armhole Edge Increase Row every 4th row 7 (7, 5, 5, 3, 2) more times, then every 6th row 0 (0, 2, 2, 4, 5) times.

Upon completion of this section, you will have worked the Armhole Increase Row a total of 8 times; you now have 90 (96, 102, 108, 114, 120) stitches on your needle.

Work 3 (3, 3, 5, 5, 5) rows even in established pattern or until armhole measures 6½ (7, 7¾, 8, 8¾, 9)" from marked row, ending with a WS row.

SHAPE SHOULDERS AND BACK NECK

Please review Sloped Bind Off and Binding Off Over Cabled Fabrics (see Special Techniques) before proceeding. Bind off stitches in pattern.

Bind off 4 (5, 4, 5, 5, 6) stitches at the beginning of the next 4 rows, then bind off 4 (4, 5, 5, 6, 6) stitches at the beginning of the next 4 rows. [58 (60, 66, 68, 70, 72) stitches remain]

Next Row (RS): Bind off 4 (4, 5, 5, 6, 6) stitches, work 17 (18, 19, 20, 20, 21) stitches as established (including last stitch from bind-off) then transfer these stitches to stitch holder or waste yarn for right shoulder, bind off 16 (16, 18, 18, 18, 18) stitches, work as established to end. [21 (22, 24, 25, 26, 27) stitches remain for left shoulder]

LEFT SHOULDER

Next Row (WS): Bind off 4 (4, 5, 5, 6, 6) stitches, work as established to end. [17 (18, 19, 20, 20, 21) stitches remain]

Next Row (RS): Bind off 14 (14, 14, 14, 15, 15) stitches, work as established to end. [3 (4, 5, 6, 5, 6) stitches remain]

Bind off remaining stitches.

RIGHT SHOULDER

Return held 17 (18, 19, 20, 20, 21) stitches to Size A needle and rejoin yarn ready to work a WS row.

Next Row (WS): Bind off 14 (14, 14, 14, 15, 15) stitches, work as established to end. [3 (4, 5, 6, 5, 6) stitches remain]

Bind off remaining stitches.

FRONT

Work as for back to last Armhole Edge Increase Row. [90 (96, 102, 108, 114, 120) stitches now on needle]

Work 1 row even (WS). Armhole measures approximately 6¼ (6¾, 7½, 7¼, 8, 8¼)" from marked row.

SHAPE SHOULDERS AND FRONT NECK

Use the Sloped Bind Off and work according to Binding Off Over Cabled Fabrics where applicable in this section for best results. Bind off stitches in pattern.

Next Row (RS): Work 37 (40, 42, 45, 48, 51) stitches as established then transfer these stitches to stitch holder or waste yarn for left shoulder, bind off 16 (16, 18, 18, 18, 18) stitches, work as established to end. [37 (40, 42, 45, 48, 51) stitches remain for right shoulder]

RIGHT SHOULDER

Next Row (WS): Work even as established.
Next Row (RS): Bind off 5 stitches, work as established to end. [32 (35, 37, 40, 43, 46) stitches remain]

Sizes 48¼, 51¾, & 55¾" Only:
Next Row (WS): Work even as established.
Next Row (RS): Bind off 4 stitches, work as established to end. [– (–, –, 36, 39, 42) stitches remain]

All Sizes Resume:
Row 1 (WS): Bind off 4 (5, 4, 5, 5, 6) stitches, work as established to end. [28 (30, 33, 31, 34, 36) stitches remain]
Row 2 (RS): Bind off 4 (4, 4, 2, 3, 3) stitches, work as established to end. [24 (26, 29, 29, 31, 33) stitches remain]
Row 3: Repeat Row 1. [20 (21, 25, 24, 26, 27) stitches remain]
Row 4: Bind off 3 (3, 3, 1, 1, 1) stitch(es), work as established to end. [17 (18, 22, 23, 25, 26) stitches remain]
Row 5: Bind off 4 (4, 5, 5, 6, 6) stitches, work as established to end. [13 (14, 17, 18, 19, 20) stitches remain]
Row 6: Bind off 1 stitch, work as established to end. [12 (13, 16, 17, 18, 19) stitches remain]
Rows 7 & 8: Repeat Rows 5 & 6. [7 (8, 10, 11, 11, 12) stitches remain]
Row 9: Repeat Row 5. [3 (4, 5, 6, 5, 6) stitches remain]
Row 10: Work even as established.

Bind off remaining stitches.

LEFT SHOULDER

Return held 37 (40, 42, 45, 48, 51) stitches to Size A needle and rejoin yarn ready to work a WS row.

Next Row (WS): Bind off 5 stitches, work as established to end. [32 (35, 37, 40, 43, 46) stitches remain]

Sizes 48¼, 51¾, & 55¾" Only:
Next Row (RS): Work even as established.
Next Row (WS): Bind off 4 stitches, work as established to end. [– (–, –, 36, 39, 42) stitches remain]

All Sizes Resume:

Row 1 (RS): Bind off 4 (5, 4, 5, 5, 6) stitches, work as established to end. [28 (30, 33, 31, 34, 36) stitches remain]

Row 2 (WS): Bind off 4 (4, 4, 2, 3, 3) stitches, work as established to end. [24 (26, 29, 29, 31, 33) stitches remain]

Row 3: Repeat Row 1. [20 (21, 25, 24, 26, 27) stitches remain]

Row 4: Bind off 3 (3, 3, 1, 1, 1) stitch(es), work as established to end. [17 (18, 22, 23, 25, 26) stitches remain]

Row 5: Bind off 4 (4, 5, 5, 6, 6) stitches, work as established to end. [13 (14, 17, 18, 19, 20) stitches remain]

Row 6: Bind off 1 stitch, work as established to end. [12 (13, 16, 17, 18, 19) stitches remain]

Rows 7 & 8: Repeat Rows 5 & 6. [7 (8, 10, 11, 11, 12) stitches remain]

Row 9: Repeat Row 5. [3 (4, 5, 6, 5, 6) stitches remain]

Row 10: Work even as established.

Bind off remaining stitches.

SLEEVES (MAKE 2)

With Size B needle(s) cast on 32 (32, 32, 36, 36, 36) stitches using your preferred method.

WORK RIBBING

Begin 2x2 Ribbing; work even until piece measures approximately 3" from cast-on edge, ending with a WS row.

BEGIN MAIN PATTERN

Switch to Size A needle(s).

Next Row (RS): {Knit 1}, work Row 1 of Welt Pattern to last stitch, {knit 1}.

Next Row (WS): {Knit 1}, work Row 2 of Welt Pattern to last stitch, {knit 1}.

Work even in established pattern for 2 more rows, ending with a WS row.

SHAPE SLEEVE

Sleeve Increase Row (RS): {Knit 1}, work 2 stitches in pattern, M1R (or M1P to keep in pattern), work to last 3 stitches, M1L (or M1P to keep in pattern), work 2 stitches in pattern, {knit 1}. (2 stitches increased)

Repeat the Sleeve Increase Row every 18th (12th, 10th, 10th, 8th, 6th) row 4 (6, 4, 4, 4, 11) more times, then every 0 (0, 8th, 8th, 6th, 0) row 0 (0, 4, 4, 6, 0) times.

Upon completion of this section, you will have worked the Sleeve Increase Row a total of 5 (7, 9, 9, 11, 12) times; you now have 42 (46, 50, 54, 58, 60) stitches on your needle.

Work even until piece measures 18½ (18½, 18½, 18½, 18, 17½)" from cast-on edge, ending with Row 4 of pattern.

Bind off all stitches.

Repeat instructions for second sleeve.

FINISHING

Wet-block pieces to schematic measurements (see *Special Techniques*), leaving removable markers or coilless safety pins in place.

With matching firmly spun yarn threaded on a tapestry needle, sew shoulder seams (see *Construction Notes*).

Sew sleeves to armhole edges between removable markers or coilless safety pins, matching center of sleeve to shoulder seam. Remove markers. Sew side and sleeve seams.

NECKBAND

With Size B 16" circular needle, RS facing, and beginning at right shoulder seam, pick up and knit 44 (44, 46, 46, 48, 48) stitches along back neck edge and 52 (52, 54, 54, 56, 56) stitches along front neck edge. Place marker for BOR and join for working in the round. [96 (96, 100, 100, 104, 104) stitches now on needle]

Next Round: *Knit 2, purl 2; repeat from * to end.

Repeat the last round until neckband measures approximately 1". Bind off all stitches in pattern.

Weave in ends. Steam neckband and seams gently or wet-block entire garment again.

HAGUE

CHART

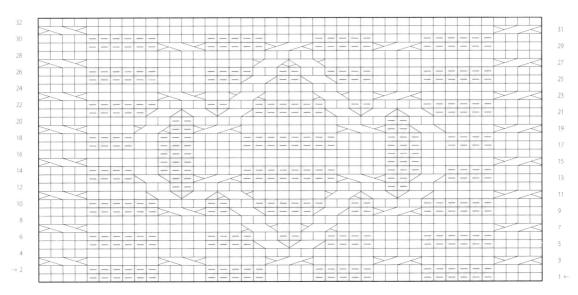

42-stitch panel
32-row repeat

	Knit
	Knit stitch on RS; purl stitch on WS

	Purl
—	Purl stitch on RS; knit stitch on WS

2/2 LC (Left Cross)
Slip 2 stitches to CN and hold in front, knit 2 stitches from
L needle, knit 2 stitches from CN

2/2 RC (Right Cross)
Slip 2 stitches to CN and hold in back, knit 2 stitches from
L needle, knit 2 stitches from CN

2/1 LT (Left Twist)
Slip 2 stitches to CN and hold in front, purl 1 stitch from
L needle, knit 2 stitches from CN

2/1 RT (Right Twist)
Slip 1 stitch to CN and hold in back, knit 2 stitches from
L needle, purl stitch from CN

2/1 LC
Slip 2 stitches to CN and hold in front, knit 1 stitch from
L needle, knit 2 stitches from CN

2/1 RC
Slip 1 stitch to CN and hold in back, knit 2 stitches from
L needle, knit stitch from CN

RADMERE

OVERVIEW

SCHEMATIC
67

PATTERN
68

CHARTS
75

MATERIALS

1905 (2050, 2325, 2530, 2855, 3040) yards of worsted weight wool yarn

14 (15, 17, 19, 21, 22) skeins of Brooklyn Tweed *Shelter* (100% American Targhee-Columbia wool; 140 yards/50 grams)

Photographed in color *Hayloft*

GAUGE

25 stitches & 28 rows = 4" in chart patterns with Size A needle(s), after blocking

18 stitches & 28 rows = 4" in stockinette stitch with Size A needle(s), after blocking

NEEDLES

Size A (for Main Fabric)
One 32" circular needle in size needed to obtain gauge listed
Suggested Size: 5 mm (US 8)
Size B (for Ribbing)
One 40" circular needle, two sizes smaller than Size A
Suggested Size: 4 mm (US 6)

Lavish cables and a modern fit for sartorial splendor. Banish chilly drafts and wardrobe tedium with this striking shawl-collared cardigan.

ADDITIONAL TOOLS

Stitch markers, locking markers or coilless safety pins, stitch holders or waste yarn, cable needle (CN), T-pins (optional), blunt tapestry needle, five 1" buttons, a small amount of sock yarn in a similar color for seaming

FINISHED DIMENSIONS

41½ (44¾, 49¼, 52½, 57¼, 60¾)" [105.5 (113.5, 125, 133.5, 145.5, 154.5) cm] circumference at chest, buttoned
Intended Ease: + 3–5" [7.5–12.5 cm]
Sample shown is size 44¾" [113.5 cm] with 6¾" [17 cm] ease on model

SKILL LEVEL

● ● ● ● ●

CONSTRUCTION NOTES

The cardigan is worked in pieces from the bottom up and sewn together. The collar stitches are picked up around the front edges and back neck edge. The collar is then worked flat and shaped using Short Rows: Turn & Slip Method (see *Special Techniques*).

The Sloped Bind Off (see *Special Techniques*) is used when shaping the armholes, shoulders, and sleeve caps.

Read RS (odd-numbered) chart rows from right to left; read WS (even-numbered) chart rows from left to right. Review the charts carefully as multiple charts are combined on each piece.

The chart includes left and right cable crosses (LC and RC) where knit stitches are crossed over knit stitches and left and right cable twists (LT and RT) where knit stitches are crossed over purl stitches.

While working shaping or when a start/end point for your size intersects a cable, if you do not have enough stitches to complete the cable, work the affected stitches as knit or purl as they appear.

Each size has a slightly different cable pattern setup at the side edges of the body.

Where {knit 1} appears in braces, it indicates a selvedge stitch.

Pieces are worked flat on a circular needle to accommodate the large number of stitches. A longer Size B needle is required due to the width of the collar.

RADMERE

SCHEMATIC

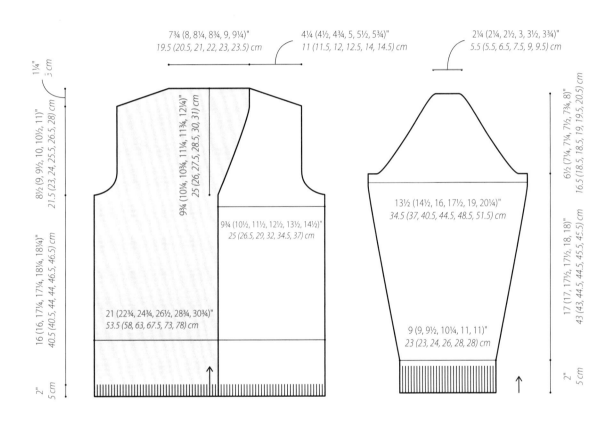

7¾ (8, 8¼, 8¾, 9, 9¼)"
19.5 (20.5, 21, 22, 23, 23.5) cm

4¼ (4½, 4¾, 5, 5½, 5¾)"
11 (11.5, 12, 12.5, 14, 14.5) cm

2¼ (2¼, 2½, 3, 3½, 3¾)"
5.5 (5.5, 6.5, 7.5, 9, 9.5) cm

1¼"
3 cm

8½ (9, 9½, 10, 10½, 11)"
21.5 (23, 24, 25.5, 26.5, 28) cm

9¾ (10¼, 10¾, 11¼, 11¾, 12¼)"
25 (26, 27.5, 28.5, 30, 31) cm

9¾ (10½, 11½, 12½, 13½, 14½)"
25 (26.5, 29, 32, 34.5, 37) cm

6½ (7¼, 7¼, 7½, 7¾, 8)"
16.5 (18.5, 18.5, 19, 19.5, 20.5) cm

13½ (14½, 16, 17½, 19, 20¼)"
34.5 (37, 40.5, 44.5, 48.5, 51.5) cm

16 (16, 17¼, 17¼, 18¼, 18¼)"
40.5 (40.5, 44, 44, 46.5, 46.5) cm

17 (17, 17½, 17½, 18, 18)"
43 (43, 44.5, 44.5, 45.5, 45.5) cm

21 (22¾, 24¾, 26½, 28¾, 30¾)"
53.5 (58, 63, 67.5, 73, 78) cm

9 (9, 9½, 10¼, 11, 11)"
23 (23, 24, 26, 28, 28) cm

2"
5 cm

2"
5 cm

RADMERE

STITCH PATTERN

2X2 RIBBING
Multiple of 4 stitches + 2; 2-row repeat

Row 1 (RS): {Knit 1}, knit 1, purl 2, *knit 2, purl 2; repeat from * to last 2 stitches, knit 1, {knit 1}.
Row 2 (WS): {Knit 1}, purl 1, knit 2, *purl 2, knit 2; repeat from * to last 2 stitches, purl 1, {knit 1}.

BACK

With Size B 40" circular needle (suggested size: 4 mm/ US 6) cast on 126 (138, 150, 162, 174, 186) stitches using your preferred method. Do not join; work back and forth in rows.

WORK RIBBING
Begin 2x2 Ribbing (see *Stitch Pattern*); work even until piece measures approximately 2" from cast-on edge, ending with a WS row.

BEGIN MAIN PATTERN
Switch to Size A 32" circular needle (suggested size: 5 mm/ US 8).

Note: On the following row, begin with Row 1 of each chart. Please note that all charts are not worked for all sizes; take care to read the brackets carefully.

Next Row (RS): {Knit 1}, purl 8 (6, 7, 6, 9, 8), [place marker, work Right Rope Chart over 4 stitches, place marker, purl 1] 0 (0, 1, 1, 0, 0) time(s), [place marker, work Right Asymmetrical Braid Chart over 14 stitches, place marker, purl 1] 0 (0, 0, 0, 1, 1) time(s), [place marker, work Right Small Braid Chart over 6 stitches, place marker, purl 1] 1 (0, 0, 1, 0, 1) time(s), [place marker, work Right Asymmetrical Braid Chart over 14 stitches, place marker, purl 1] 0 (1, 1, 1, 1, 1) time(s), place marker, work Interlocking Chart over 36 stitches, place marker, purl 1, place marker, work Center Chart over 20 stitches, place marker, purl 1, place marker, work Interlocking Chart over 36 stitches, place marker, purl 1, [place marker, work Left Asymmetrical Braid Chart over 14 stitches, place marker, purl 1] 0 (1, 1, 1, 1, 1) time(s), [place marker, work Left Small Braid Chart over 6 stitches, place marker, purl 1] 1 (0, 0, 1, 0, 1) time(s), [place marker, work Left Asymmetrical Braid Chart over 14 stitches, place marker, purl 1] 0 (0, 0, 0, 1, 1) time(s), [place marker, work Left Rope Chart over 4 stitches, place marker, purl 1] 0 (0, 1, 1, 0, 0) time(s), purl 7 (5, 6, 5, 8, 7), {knit 1}.

Work even, working charts between markers as established, background stitches in reverse stockinette stitch (purl on RS; knit on WS), and each selvedge stitch in garter stitch (knit every row) until piece measures 18 (18, 19¼, 19¼, 20¼, 20¼)" from cast-on edge, ending with a WS row.

SHAPE ARMHOLES

Please review Sloped Bind Off and Binding Off Over Cabled Fabrics (see Special Techniques) before proceeding. Bind off in pattern.

Bind off 5 (6, 7, 8, 9, 10) stitches at the beginning of the next 2 rows, then bind off 4 stitches at the beginning of the next 2 rows, then bind off 2 (3, 3, 3, 3, 3) stitches at the beginning of the next 2 rows, then bind off 0 (2, 2, 2, 2, 2) stitches at the beginning of the next 0 (2, 2, 2, 2, 2) rows, then bind off 1 stitch at the beginning of the next 4 (2, 6, 10, 14, 18) rows. [100 (106, 112, 118, 124, 130) stitches remain]

Once bind-offs are complete, maintain pattern as follows beginning with next RS row:

For Size 41½" Only: {Knit 1}, purl 2, work charts as established over center 94 stitches, purl 2, {knit 1}.

For Size 44¾" Only: Maintain pattern as established if necessary until Row 20 of Right and Left Asymmetrical Braid Charts is complete. Thereafter: {Knit 1}, knit 2, purl 3, work charts as established over center 94 stitches, purl 3, knit 2, {knit 1}.

For Size 49¼, 52½, & 57¼" Only: {Knit 1}, maintain chart pattern over next – (–, 7, 10, 13, –) stitches, purl 1, work charts as established over center 94 stitches, purl 1, maintain chart pattern over next – (–, 7, 10, 13, –) stitches, {knit 1}.

For Size 60¾" Only: {Knit 1}, purl 2, work charts as established over center 124 stitches, purl 2, {knit 1}.

Work even as established until armholes measure 8½ (9, 9½, 10, 10½, 11)", ending with a WS row.

SHAPE SHOULDERS

Note: Use the Sloped Bind Off and work according to Binding Off Over Cabled Fabrics for best results. Bind off in pattern.

Bind off 6 (7, 8, 8, 9, 9) stitches at the beginning of the next 4 rows, then bind off 7 (7, 7, 8, 8, 9) stitches at the beginning of the following 4 rows. [48 (50, 52, 54, 56, 58) stitches remain]

Bind off remaining stitches.

LEFT FRONT

With Size B 40" circular needle cast on 56 (62, 68, 74, 80, 86) stitches using your preferred method.

WORK RIBBING

Begin 2x2 Ribbing; work even until piece measures approximately 2" from cast-on edge, ending with a WS row.

BEGIN MAIN PATTERN

Switch to Size A 32" circular needle.

Note: On the following row, begin with Row 1 of each chart. Please note that all charts are not worked for all sizes; take care to read the brackets carefully.

Next Row (RS): {Knit 1}, purl 8 (6, 7, 6, 9, 8), [place marker, work Right Rope Chart over 4 stitches, place marker, purl 1] 0 (0, 1, 1, 0, 0) time(s), [place marker, work Right Asymmetrical Braid Chart over 14 stitches, place marker, purl 1] 0 (0, 0, 0, 1, 1) time(s), [place marker, work Right Small Braid Chart over 6 stitches, place marker, purl 1] 1 (0, 0, 1, 0, 1) time(s), [place marker, work Right Asymmetrical Braid Chart over 14 stitches, place marker, purl 1] 0 (1, 1, 1, 1, 1) time(s), place marker, work Interlocking Chart over 36 stitches, place marker, purl 1, knit 2, {knit 1}.

Work even, working charts between markers as established, background stitches in reverse stockinette stitch, and each selvedge stitch in garter stitch until piece measures 18 (18, 19¼, 19¼, 20¼, 20¼)" from cast-on edge, ending with a WS row.

SHAPE NECK AND ARMHOLE

Note: Neck and armhole shaping are worked at the same time. Please read the following section through to the end before proceeding. Please review Sloped Bind Off and Binding Off Over Cabled Fabrics before proceeding. Bind off in pattern and re-establish {knit 1} at armhole edge once bind-offs are complete.

Decrease Row (RS): Bind off 5 (6, 7, 8, 9, 10) stitches, work as established to last 5 stitches, SSK (or SSP to keep in pattern), knit 2, {knit 1}. [5 (6, 7, 8, 9, 10) stitches bound off at armhole edge; 1 stitch decreased at neck edge]

Next Row (WS): {Knit 1}, purl 3, work as established to end.

At the beginning of RS rows, bind off 4 stitches once, then bind off 2 (3, 3, 3, 3, 3) stitches once, then bind off 0 (2, 2, 2, 2, 2) stitches 0 (1, 1, 1, 1, 1) time(s), then bind off 1 stitch 2 (1, 3, 5, 7, 9) time(s) and, AT THE SAME TIME, decrease 1 stitch at neck edge (as before) every RS row 3 (4, 4, 4, 5, 5) more times, then every 4th row 13 (13, 14, 15, 15, 16) times. Maintain pattern as established over remaining stitches, working stitches near the armhole edge the same as you did for the back.

Upon completion of this section you will have bound off a total of 13 (16, 19, 22, 25, 28) stitches at armhole edge and decreased a total of 17 (18, 19, 20, 21, 22) stitches at neck edge; you will have 26 (28, 30, 32, 34, 36) stitches on your needle when all shaping is complete.

Work even as established until armhole measures 8½ (9, 9½, 10, 10½, 11)", ending with a WS row.

SHAPE SHOULDER

Note: Use the Sloped Bind Off and work according to Binding Off Over Cabled Fabrics for best results. Bind off in pattern.

Bind off 6 (7, 8, 8, 9, 9) stitches at the beginning of the next 2 RS rows, then bind off 7 (7, 7, 8, 8, 9) stitches at the beginning of the following RS row. [7 (7, 7, 8, 8, 9) stitches remain]

Bind off remaining stitches on next RS row.

RIGHT FRONT

With Size B 40" circular needle cast on 56 (62, 68, 74, 80, 86) stitches using your preferred method.

WORK RIBBING

Begin 2x2 Ribbing; work even until piece measures approximately 2" from cast-on edge, ending with a WS row.

BEGIN MAIN PATTERN

Switch to Size A 32" circular needle.

Note: On the following row, begin with Row 1 of each chart. Please note that all charts are not worked for all sizes; take care to read the brackets carefully.

Next Row (RS): {Knit 1}, knit 2, purl 1, place marker, work Interlocking Chart over 36 stitches, place marker, purl 1, [place marker, work Left Asymmetrical Braid Chart over 14 stitches, place marker, purl 1] 0 (1, 1, 1, 1, 1) time(s), [place marker, work Left Small Braid Chart over 6 stitches, place marker, purl 1] 1 (0, 0, 1, 0, 1) time(s), [place marker,

work Left Asymmetrical Braid Chart over 14 stitches, place marker, purl 1] 0 (0, 0, 0, 1, 1) time(s), [place marker, work Left Rope Chart over 4 stitches, place marker, purl 1] 0 (0, 1, 1, 0, 0) time(s), purl 7 (5, 6, 5, 8, 7), {knit 1}.

Work even, working charts between markers as established, background stitches in reverse stockinette stitch, and each selvedge stitch in garter stitch until piece measures 18 (18, 19¼, 19¼, 20¼, 20¼)" from cast-on edge, ending with a WS row.

SHAPE NECK AND ARMHOLE

Note: Neck and armhole shaping are worked at the same time. Please read the following section through to the end before proceeding. Please review Sloped Bind Off and Binding Off Over Cabled Fabrics before proceeding. Bind off in pattern and re-establish {knit 1} at armhole edge once bind-offs are complete.

Neck Decrease Row (RS): {Knit 1}, knit 2, k2tog, work as established to end. (1 stitch decreased)

Next Row (WS): Bind off 5 (6, 7, 8, 9, 10) stitches, work as established to last 4 stitches, purl 3, {knit 1}.

Decrease 1 stitch at neck edge (as before) every RS row 3 (4, 4, 4, 5, 5) more times, then every 4th row 13 (13, 14, 15, 15, 16) times and AT THE SAME TIME, at the beginning of WS rows, bind off 4 stitches once, then bind off 2 (3, 3, 3, 3, 3) stitches once, then bind off 0 (2, 2, 2, 2, 2) stitches 0 (1, 1, 1, 1, 1) time(s), then bind off 1 stitch 2 (1, 3, 5, 7, 9) time(s). Maintain pattern as established over remaining stitches, working stitches near the armhole edge the same as you did for the back.

Upon completion of this section you will have bound off a total of 13 (16, 19, 22, 25, 28) stitches at armhole edge and decreased a total of 17 (18, 19, 20, 21, 22) stitches at neck edge; you will have 26 (28, 30, 32, 34, 36) stitches on your needle when all shaping is complete.

Work even as established until armhole measures 8½ (9, 9½, 10, 10½, 11)", ending with a RS row.

SHAPE SHOULDER

Note: Use the Sloped Bind Off and work according to Binding Off Over Cabled Fabrics for best results. Bind off in pattern.

Bind off 6 (7, 8, 8, 9, 9) stitches at the beginning of the next 2 WS rows, then bind off 7 (7, 7, 8, 8, 9) stitches at the beginning of the following WS row. [7 (7, 7, 8, 8, 9) stitches remain]

Bind off remaining stitches on next WS row.

SLEEVES (MAKE 2)

With Size B 40" circular needle cast on 56 (56, 60, 64, 68, 68) stitches using your preferred method.

WORK RIBBING

Next Row (RS): {Knit 1}, knit 2, *purl 2, knit 2; repeat from * to last stitch, {knit 1}.
Next Row (WS): {Knit 1}, purl 2, *knit 2, purl 2; repeat from * to last stitch, {knit 1}.

Repeat the last 2 rows until piece measures approximately 2" from cast-on edge, ending with a WS row.

BEGIN MAIN PATTERN

Switch to Size A 32" circular needle.

Note: On the following row, begin with Row 1 of each chart.

Next Row (RS): {Knit 1}, beginning where indicated for your size, work Right Side Sleeve Chart over 15 (15, 17, 19, 21, 21) stitches, place marker, purl 2, place marker, work Center Chart over 20 stitches, place marker, purl 2, place marker, work Left Side Sleeve Chart over 15 (15, 17, 19, 21, 21) stitches ending where indicated for your size, {knit 1}.

Work even, working charts between markers as established, background stitches in reverse stockinette stitch, and each selvedge stitch in garter stitch for 5 more rows, ending with a WS row.

SHAPE SLEEVE

Sleeve Increase Row (RS): {Knit 1}, M1R (or M1P to keep in pattern), work as established to last stitch, M1L (or M1P to keep in pattern), {knit 1}. (2 stitches increased)

Repeat the Sleeve Increase Row every 8th (6th, 6th, 6th, 6th, 4th) row 9 (16, 11, 5, 3, 23) more times, then every 6th (0, 4th, 4th, 4th, 2nd) row 4 (0, 8, 17, 21, 5) times, working new stitches into Right and Left Side Sleeve Chart patterns.

Upon completion of this section, you will have worked the Sleeve Increase Row a total of 14 (17, 20, 23, 25, 29) times; you now have 84 (90, 100, 110, 118, 126) stitches on your needle.

Work even in established pattern until piece measures
19 (19, 19½, 19½, 20, 20)" from cast-on edge, ending with a
WS row.

SHAPE SLEEVE CAP
*Use the Sloped Bind Off and work according to Binding Off
Over Cabled Fabrics for best results. Bind off in pattern.*

Bind off 5 (6, 7, 8, 9, 10) stitches at the beginning of the next
2 rows, then bind off 3 (3, 4, 5, 5, 5) stitches at the beginning
of the following 2 rows, then bind off 0 (0, 2, 2, 2, 2) stitches
at the beginning of the next 0 (0, 4, 6, 6, 8) rows. [68 (72, 70,
72, 78, 80) stitches remain]

Bind off 1 stitch at the beginning of the next 38 (42, 38, 38,
40, 40) rows, then bind off 4 stitches at the beginning of the
next 4 rows. [14 (14, 16, 18, 22, 24) stitches remain]

Bind off remaining stitches.

FINISHING

Wet-block pieces to schematic measurements (see *Special
Techniques*). With matching sock yarn threaded on a tapestry
needle, sew shoulder seams.

COLLAR

With Size B 40" circular needle, RS facing, and beginning at bottom of right front, pick up and knit 94 (94, 102, 102, 106, 106) stitches up right front edge to first neck decrease, place marker, 63 (66, 67, 72, 73, 78) stitches up right neck edge to shoulder seam, 48 (50, 52, 54, 56, 58) stitches along back neck, 63 (66, 67, 72, 73, 78) stitches down left neck edge to first neck decrease, place marker, and 94 (94, 102, 102, 106, 106) stitches down left front edge ending at bottom edge. [362 (370, 390, 402, 414, 426) stitches now on needle]

Next Row (WS): Slip 1 purlwise wyif, purl 1, *knit 2, purl 2; repeat from * to end.

Note: Please Review Short Rows: Turn & Slip Method (see Special Techniques*) before proceeding.*

Short Row 1 (RS): Slip 1 purlwise wyib, [work in established rib pattern to marker, slip marker] twice, work 1 stitch in rib, turn & slip;

Short Row 2 (WS): Slip marker, work in established rib pattern to marker, slip marker, work 1 stitch in rib, turn & slip;

Short Row 3: Work in established rib pattern to 5 (6, 6, 6, 6, 7) stitches before gap from previous RS row, turn & slip;

Short Row 4: Work in established rib pattern to 5 (6, 6, 6, 6, 7) stitches before gap from previous WS row, turn & slip;

Short Rows 5–20: Repeat Short Rows 3 & 4 eight more times.

Next Row (RS): Work in established rib pattern to end, closing gaps as you go as described in *Special Techniques*.
Next Row (WS): Work in established rib pattern to end, closing remaining gaps as you go.

Work 2 rows even in established rib pattern, ending with a WS row.

Buttonhole Row (RS): [Work to marker, slip marker] twice, work 2 (2, 4, 4, 4, 4) stitches in rib, work 4-stitch One-Row Buttonhole (see *Special Techniques*), *work 17 (17, 18, 18, 19, 19) stitches in rib, work 4-stitch One-Row Buttonhole; repeat from * 3 more times, work last 4 (4, 6, 6, 6, 6) stitches in rib.

Work 1 row even (WS).

Repeat Short Rows 1–20 once more.

Next Row (RS): Work in established rib pattern to end, closing gaps as you go.
Next Row (WS): Work in established rib pattern to end, closing remaining gaps as you go.

Work even in established rib for 4 more rows, ending with a WS row.

Bind off all stitches in pattern.

Sew side and sleeve seams. Set in sleeves. Weave in ends. Steam collar and seams gently or wet-block entire garment again. Sew on buttons to correspond to buttonholes.

RADMERE

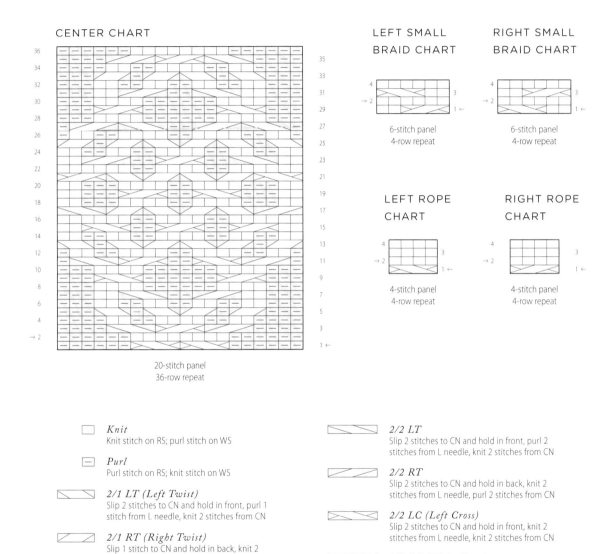

CENTER CHART

20-stitch panel
36-row repeat

LEFT SMALL BRAID CHART

6-stitch panel
4-row repeat

RIGHT SMALL BRAID CHART

6-stitch panel
4-row repeat

LEFT ROPE CHART

4-stitch panel
4-row repeat

RIGHT ROPE CHART

4-stitch panel
4-row repeat

Knit
Knit stitch on RS; purl stitch on WS

Purl
Purl stitch on RS; knit stitch on WS

2/1 LT (Left Twist)
Slip 2 stitches to CN and hold in front, purl 1 stitch from L needle, knit 2 stitches from CN

2/1 RT (Right Twist)
Slip 1 stitch to CN and hold in back, knit 2 stitches from L needle, purl stitch from CN

2/2 LT
Slip 2 stitches to CN and hold in front, purl 2 stitches from L needle, knit 2 stitches from CN

2/2 RT
Slip 2 stitches to CN and hold in back, knit 2 stitches from L needle, purl 2 stitches from CN

2/2 LC (Left Cross)
Slip 2 stitches to CN and hold in front, knit 2 stitches from L needle, knit 2 stitches from CN

2/2 RC (Right Cross)
Slip 2 stitches to CN and hold in back, knit 2 stitches from L needle, knit 2 stitches from CN

RADMERE

RIGHT ASYMMETRICAL BRAID CHART

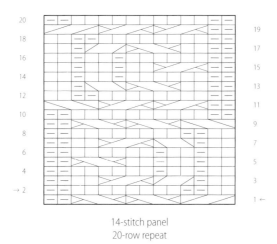

14-stitch panel
20-row repeat

LEFT ASYMMETRICAL BRAID CHART

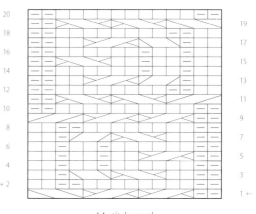

14-stitch panel
20-row repeat

INTERLOCKING CHART

36-stitch panel
28-row repeat

RADMERE

RIGHT SIDE SLEEVE CHART

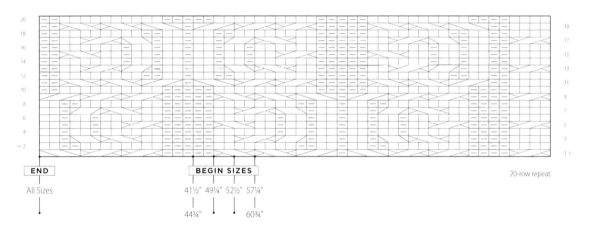

END

All Sizes

BEGIN SIZES

41½" 49¼" 52½" 57¼"

44¾" 60¾"

20-row repeat

LEFT SIDE SLEEVE CHART

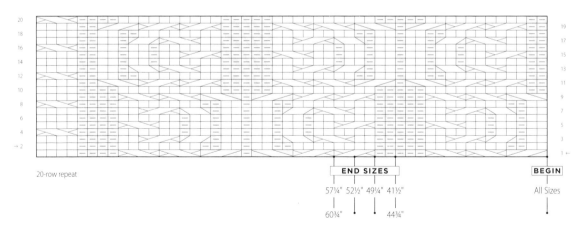

20-row repeat

END SIZES

57¼" 52½" 49¼" 41½"

60¾" 44¾"

BEGIN

All Sizes

PALMER

OVERVIEW

SCHEMATIC
80

PATTERN
81

MATERIALS
2250 (2500, 2800, 3070, 3380, 3635) yards of fingering weight wool yarn
9 (10, 11, 12, 13, 14) skeins of Brooklyn Tweed *Loft* (100% American Targhee-Columbia wool; 275 yards/50 grams)

Photographed in color *Woodsmoke*

GAUGE
23 stitches & 34 rows = 4" in stockinette stitch with Size A needle(s), after blocking

NEEDLES
Size A (for Main Fabric)
One pair of straight needles or a 24" circular needle* in size needed to obtain gauge listed
Suggested Size: 3¾ mm (US 5)
Size B (for Ribbing)
One pair of straight needles or a 24" circular needle* and one 47" circular needle, two sizes smaller than Size A
Suggested Size: 3¼ mm (US 3)
Knitter's preferred style of needle may be used

Breathing room. Find tranquility in the meditative stockinette and pure, uncluttered design of this minimalist cardigan.

ADDITIONAL TOOLS

Stitch markers, cable needle (CN), stitch holders or waste yarn, T-pins (optional), blunt tapestry needle, a small amount of sock yarn in a similar color for seaming (see *Construction Notes*)

FINISHED DIMENSIONS

36 (40, 44, 48½, 52½, 56½)" [91.5 (101.5, 112, 123, 133.5, 143.5) cm] circumference at bust, with fronts overlapping approximately 1" [2.5 cm]

Intended Ease: + 4–6" [10–15 cm]

Sample shown is size 40" [101.5 cm] with 6" [15 cm] ease on model

SKILL LEVEL

● ● ● ○ ○

CONSTRUCTION NOTES

The pieces are worked flat from the bottom up and sewn together. The collar is picked up along the front edges and back neck edge and worked flat.

Where {knit 1} appears in braces, it indicates a selvedge stitch.

The Sloped Bind Off (see *Special Techniques*) is used when shaping the armholes and sleeve caps.

Because of the softly spun nature of *Loft*, some knitters prefer to do their seaming with a firmly spun yarn, such as sock yarn, in a similar color; alternatively, you may add twist into the yarn (in the same direction as the yarn is plied) as you seam to add tensile strength.

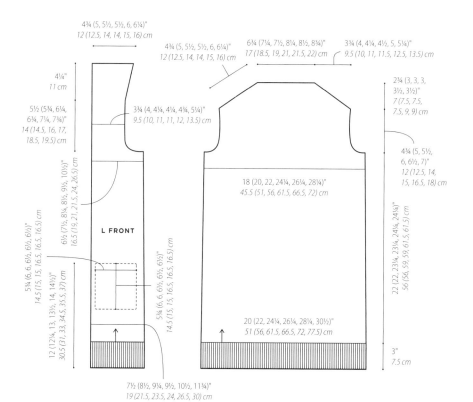

4¾ (5, 5½, 5½, 6, 6¼)"
12 (12.5, 14, 14, 15, 16) cm

4¾ (5, 5½, 5½, 6, 6¼)"
12 (12.5, 14, 14, 15, 16) cm

6¾ (7¼, 7½, 8¼, 8½, 8¾)"
17 (18.5, 19, 21, 21.5, 22) cm

3¾ (4, 4¼, 4½, 5, 5¼)"
9.5 (10, 11, 11.5, 12.5, 13.5) cm

4¼"
11 cm

5½ (5¾, 6¼, 6¾, 7¼, 7¾)"
14 (14.5, 16, 17, 18.5, 19.5) cm

3¾ (4, 4¼, 4¼, 4¾, 5¼)"
9.5 (10, 11, 11, 12, 13.5) cm

2¾ (3, 3, 3, 3½, 3½)"
7 (7.5, 7.5, 7.5, 9, 9) cm

4¾ (5, 5½, 6, 6½, 7)"
12 (12.5, 14, 15, 16.5, 18) cm

6½ (7½, 8¼, 8½, 9½, 10½)"
16.5 (19, 21, 21.5, 24, 26.5) cm

L FRONT

18 (20, 22, 24¼, 26¼, 28¼)"
45.5 (51, 56, 61.5, 66.5, 72) cm

22 (22, 23¼, 23¾, 24¼, 24¼)"
56 (56, 59, 59, 61.5, 61.5) cm

5¾ (6, 6, 6½, 6½)"
14.5 (15, 15, 16.5, 16.5) cm

5¾ (6, 6, 6½, 6½)"
14.5 (15, 15, 16.5, 16.5) cm

12 (12¼, 13, 13½, 14, 14½)"
30.5 (31, 33, 34.5, 35.5, 37) cm

20 (22, 24¼, 26¼, 28¼, 30½)"
51 (56, 61.5, 66.5, 72, 77.5) cm

3"
7.5 cm

7½ (8½, 9¼, 9½, 10½, 11¾)"
19 (21.5, 23.5, 24, 26.5, 30) cm

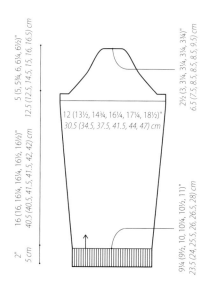

5 (5, 5¾, 6, 6¼, 6½)"
12.5 (12.5, 14.5, 15, 16, 16.5) cm

12 (13½, 14¾, 16¼, 17¼, 18½)"
30.5 (34.5, 37.5, 41.5, 44, 47) cm

2½ (3, 3¼, 3¼, 3¼, 3¾)"
6.5 (7.5, 8.5, 8.5, 8.5, 9.5) cm

16 (16, 16¼, 16¼, 16½, 16½)"
40.5 (40.5, 41.5, 41.5, 42, 42) cm

2"
5 cm

9¼ (9½, 10, 10¼, 10½, 11)"
23.5 (24, 25.5, 26, 26.5, 28) cm

PALMER

PATTERN

STITCH PATTERN

1X1 RIBBING
Odd number of stitches; 2-row repeat

Row 1 (RS): {Knit 1}, knit 1, *purl 1, knit 1; repeat from * to last stitch, {knit 1}.
Row 2 (WS): {Knit 1}, purl 1, *knit 1, purl 1; repeat from * to last stitch, {knit 1}.

Repeat Rows 1 & 2 for pattern.

POCKET LININGS (MAKE 2)

With Size A needle(s) (suggested size: 3¾ mm/US 5), cast on 33 (35, 35, 37, 37, 37) stitches using your preferred method. Do not join; work back and forth in rows.

Next Row (RS): {Knit 1}, knit to last stitch, {knit 1}.

Next Row (WS): {Knit 1}, purl to last stitch, {knit 1}.

Work even in established stockinette stitch with garter stitch selvedges until piece measures 5¾ (6, 6, 6½, 6½, 6½)" from cast-on edge, ending with a WS row. Break yarn.

Transfer stitches to stitch holder or waste yarn.

Repeat instructions for second pocket lining.

BACK

With Size B needle(s) (suggested size: 3¼ mm/US 3) cast on 115 (127, 139, 151, 163, 175) stitches using your preferred method.

WORK RIBBING
Begin 1x1 Ribbing (see *Stitch Pattern*); work even until piece measures approximately 3" from cast-on edge, ending with a WS row.

BEGIN MAIN PATTERN
Switch to Size A needle(s).

Next Row (RS): {Knit 1}, knit to last stitch, {knit 1}.

Next Row (WS): {Knit 1}, purl to last stitch, {knit 1}.

Work even in established stockinette stitch with garter stitch selvedges for 6 more rows, ending with a WS row.

SHAPE SIDES
Side Decrease Row (RS): {Knit 1}, knit 2, k2tog, knit to last 5 stitches, SSK, knit 2, {knit 1}. (2 stitches decreased)

Repeat the Side Decrease Row every 30th (30th, 32nd, 32nd, 32nd, 32nd) row 5 more times.

Upon completion of this section, you will have worked the Side Decrease Row a total of 6 times; you now have 103 (115, 127, 139, 151, 163) stitches on your needle.

Work even until piece measures 25 (25, 26¼, 26¼, 27¼, 27¼)" from cast-on edge, ending with a WS row.

SHAPE ARMHOLES

Please review Sloped Bind Off (see Special Techniques) before proceeding.

Bind off 5 (6, 7, 8, 9, 11) stitches at the beginning of the next 2 rows, then bind off 0 (4, 4, 4, 4, 4) stitches at the beginning of the following 0 (2, 2, 2, 2, 2) rows, then bind off 2 stitches at the beginning of the following 4 (2, 2, 2, 2, 2) rows, then bind off 1 stitch at the beginning of the following 4 (4, 8, 12, 14, 18) rows. [81 (87, 93, 99, 107, 111) stitches remain]

Work even (re-establishing garter stitch selvedge at each edge) until armholes measure 4¾ (5, 5½, 6, 6½, 7)", ending with a WS row.

SHAPE SHOULDERS

Sizes 36, 40, 44, & 52½" Only:

Shoulder Single Decrease Row (RS): {Knit 1}, knit 2, k2tog, knit to last 5 stitches, SSK, knit 2, {knit 1}. (2 stitches decreased)

Repeat the Shoulder Single Decrease Row every RS row 2 (2, 0, –, 0, –) more times. [75 (81, 91, –, 105, –) stitches remain]

Work 1 row even (WS).

All Sizes Resume:

Shoulder Double Decrease Row (RS): {Knit 1}, knit 2, FD2-R, knit to last 7 stitches, FD2-L, knit 2, {knit 1}. (4 stitches decreased)

Repeat the Shoulder Double Decrease Row every RS row 8 (9, 11, 12, 13, 14) more times.

Upon completion of this section, you will have worked the Shoulder Single Decrease Row a total of 3 (3, 1, 0, 1, 0) time(s), and the Shoulder Double Decrease Row a total of 9 (10, 12, 13, 14, 15) times; you now have 39 (41, 43, 47, 49, 51) stitches on your needle.

Work 1 row even (WS).

Bind off remaining stitches.

LEFT FRONT

With Size B needle(s) cast on 43 (49, 53, 55, 61, 67) stitches using your preferred method.

WORK RIBBING

Begin 1x1 Ribbing; work even until piece measures approximately 3" from cast-on edge, ending with a WS row.

BEGIN MAIN PATTERN

Switch to Size A needle(s).

Next Row (RS): {Knit 1}, knit to last stitch, {knit 1}.

Next Row (WS): {Knit 1}, purl to last stitch, {knit 1}.

Work even in established stockinette stitch with garter stitch selvedges for 6 more rows, ending with a WS row.

SHAPE SIDES AND PLACE POCKETS

Note: The sides are shaped and the pockets are placed at the same time. Please read the following section through to the end before proceeding.

Side Decrease Row (RS): {Knit 1}, knit 2, k2tog, knit to last stitch, {knit 1}. (1 stitch decreased)

Repeat the Side Decrease Row every 30th (30th, 32nd, 32nd, 32nd, 32nd) row 5 more times and, AT THE SAME TIME when piece measures 12 (12¼, 13, 13½, 14, 14½)" from cast-on edge ending with a WS row, place pockets as follows:

Pocket Placement Row (RS): {Knit 1}, work to last 36 (41, 44, 46, 49, 52) stitches, transfer next 33 (35, 35, 37, 37, 37) stitches to stitch holder or waste yarn for pocket, with RS facing, transfer 33 (35, 35, 37, 37, 37) pocket lining stitches to L needle then knit them, knit to last stitch, {knit 1}.

Upon completion of this section, you will have worked the Side Decrease Row a total of 6 times; you now have 37 (43, 47, 49, 55, 61) stitches on your needle.

Work even until piece measures 25 (25, 26¼, 26¼, 27¼, 27¼)" from cast-on edge, ending with a WS row.

SHAPE ARMHOLE

Use the Sloped Bind Off in this section for best results.

Bind off 5 (6, 7, 8, 9, 11) stitches at the beginning of the next RS row, then bind off 0 (4, 4, 4, 4, 4) stitches at the beginning of the following 0 (1, 1, 1, 1, 1) RS row(s), then bind off 2 stitches at the beginning of the following 3 (2, 2, 2, 2, 2) RS rows, then bind off 1 stitch at the beginning of the following 4 (6, 7, 8, 10, 12) RS rows. [22 (23, 25, 25, 28, 30) stitches remain]

Work even (re-establishing garter stitch selvedge at side edge) until armhole measures 5½ (5¾, 6¼, 6¾, 7¼, 7¾)", ending with a WS row.

SHAPE ARMHOLE EDGE

Armhole Increase Row (RS): {Knit 1}, knit 2, M1L, knit to last stitch, {knit 1}. (1 stitch increased)

Repeat the Armhole Increase Row every 6th row 5 more times.

Upon completion of this section, you will have worked the Armhole Increase Row a total of 6 times; you now have 28 (29, 31, 31, 34, 36) stitches on your needle.

Work even until armhole measures 9¾ (10, 10½, 11, 11½, 12)", ending with a WS row.

Bind off all stitches.

RIGHT FRONT

With Size B needle(s) cast on 43 (49, 53, 55, 61, 67) stitches using your preferred method.

WORK RIBBING
Begin 1x1 Ribbing; work even until piece measures approximately 3" from cast-on edge, ending with a WS row.

BEGIN MAIN PATTERN
Switch to Size A needle(s).

Next Row (RS): {Knit 1}, knit to last stitch, {knit 1}.

Next Row (WS): {Knit 1}, purl to last stitch, {knit 1}.

Work even in established stockinette stitch with garter stitch selvedges for 6 more rows, ending with a WS row.

SHAPE SIDES AND PLACE POCKETS
Note: The sides are shaped and the pockets are placed at the same time. Please read the following section through to the end before proceeding.

Side Decrease Row (RS): {Knit 1}, knit to last 5 stitches, SSK, knit 2, {knit 1}. (1 stitch decreased)

Repeat the Side Decrease Row every 30th (30th, 32nd, 32nd, 32nd, 32nd) row 5 more times and, AT THE SAME TIME when piece measures 12 (12¼, 13, 13½, 14, 14½)" from cast-on edge ending with a WS row, place pockets as follows:

Pocket Placement Row (RS): {Knit 1}, knit 2 (5, 8, 8, 11, 14), transfer next 33 (35, 35, 37, 37, 37) stitches to stitch holder or waste yarn for pocket, with RS facing transfer 33 (35, 35, 37, 37, 37) pocket lining stitches to L needle then knit them, knit to last stitch, {knit 1}.

Upon completion of this section, you will have worked the Side Decrease Row a total of 6 times; you now have 37 (43, 47, 49, 55, 61) stitches on your needle.

Work even until piece measures 25 (25, 26¼, 26¼, 27¼, 27¼)" from cast-on edge, ending with a RS row.

SHAPE ARMHOLE
Use the Sloped Bind Off in this section for best results.

Bind off 5 (6, 7, 8, 9, 11) stitches at the beginning of the next WS row, then bind off 0 (4, 4, 4, 4, 4) stitches at the beginning of the following 0 (1, 1, 1, 1, 1) WS row(s), then bind off 2 stitches at the beginning of the following 3 (2, 2, 2, 2, 2) WS rows, then bind off 1 stitch at the beginning of the following 4 (6, 7, 8, 10, 12) WS rows. [22 (23, 25, 25, 28, 30) stitches remain]

Work even (re-establishing garter stitch selvedge at side edge) until armhole measures 5½ (5¾, 6¼, 6¾, 7¼, 7¾)", ending with a WS row.

SHAPE ARMHOLE EDGE

Armhole Increase Row (RS): {Knit 1}, knit to last 3 stitches, M1R, knit 2, {knit 1}. (1 stitch increased)

Repeat the Armhole Increase Row every 6th row 5 more times.

Upon completion of this section, you will have worked the Armhole Increase Row a total of 6 times; you now have 28 (29, 31, 31, 34, 36) stitches on your needle.

Work even until armhole measures 9¾ (10, 10½, 11, 11½, 12)", ending with a WS row.

Bind off all stitches.

SLEEVES (MAKE 2)

With Size B needle(s) cast on 53 (55, 57, 59, 61, 63) stitches using your preferred method.

WORK RIBBING

Begin 1x1 Ribbing; work even until piece measures approximately 2" from cast-on edge, ending with a WS row.

BEGIN MAIN PATTERN

Switch to Size A needle(s).

Next Row (RS): {Knit 1}, knit to last stitch, {knit 1}.

Next Row (WS): {Knit 1}, purl to last stitch, {knit 1}.

SHAPE SLEEVE

Sleeve Increase Row (RS): {Knit 1}, knit 2, M1L, knit to last 3 stitches, M1R, knit 2, {knit 1}. (2 stitches increased)

Continuing in established stockinette stitch with garter stitch selvedges, repeat the Sleeve Increase Row every 18th (12th, 10th, 8th, 8th, 6th) row 4 (10, 9, 13, 8, 20) more times, then every 16th (0, 8th, 6th, 6th, 4th) row 3 (0, 4, 3, 10, 1) time(s).

Upon completion of this section, you will have worked the Sleeve Increase Row a total of 8 (11, 14, 17, 19, 22) times; you now have 69 (77, 85, 93, 99, 107) stitches on your needle.

Work even until piece measures 18 (18, 18¼, 18¼, 18½, 18½)" from cast-on edge, ending with a WS row.

SHAPE SLEEVE CAP

Use the Sloped Bind Off in this section for best results.

Bind off 5 (6, 7, 8, 9, 11) stitches at the beginning of the next 2 rows, then bind off 0 (0, 2, 2, 2, 2) stitches at the beginning of the following 0 (0, 2, 2, 2, 2) rows. [59 (65, 67, 73, 77, 81) stitches remain]

Cap Decrease Row (RS): {Knit 1}, knit 2, k2tog, knit to last 5 stitches, SSK, knit 2, {knit 1}. (2 stitches decreased)

Repeat the Cap Decrease Row every RS row 7 (17, 8, 20, 22, 23) more times, then every 4th row 2 (0, 2, 0, 0, 0) times, then every RS row 6 (0, 7, 0, 0, 0) times. [27 (29, 31, 31, 31, 33) stitches remain]

Next Row (WS): {Knit 1}, purl to last stitch, {knit 1}.

Bind off 3 stitches at the beginning of the next 4 rows. [15 (17, 19, 19, 19, 21) stitches remain]

Bind off all stitches.

Repeat instructions for second sleeve.

FINISHING

Wet-block pieces to schematic measurements (see *Special Techniques*).

With matching sock yarn threaded on a tapestry needle (see *Construction Notes*), sew bound-off front shoulders to sloped edge of back shoulders.

Sew side and sleeve seams. Set in sleeves.

COLLAR

With Size B 47" circular needle, RS facing, and beginning at bottom of right front, pick up and knit 177 (179, 187, 190, 198, 200) stitches up right front to shoulder seam, 39 (41, 43, 47, 49, 51) stitches along back neck edge, and 177 (179, 187, 190, 198, 200) stitches down left front to bottom edge. [393 (399, 417, 427, 445, 451) stitches now on needle]

Beginning with a WS row, work in 1x1 Ribbing until collar measures 3½ (3½, 3¾, 4½, 4½, 4½)" from pick-up row. Bind off all stitches in pattern.

POCKET EDGINGS (MAKE 2)

Transfer held 33 (35, 35, 37, 37, 37) pocket stitches to Size B needle(s). Rejoin yarn ready to work a RS row.

Begin 1x1 Ribbing; work even until edging measures 1".

Bind off all stitches in pattern.

Repeat instructions for second pocket edging.

Sew side edges of pocket edgings to RS of fronts. Sew sides and bottom of pocket linings to WS of fronts. Weave in ends. Steam collar and seams gently or wet-block entire garment again.

BINGHAM

OVERVIEW

SCHEMATIC
89

PATTERN
90

CHART
95

MATERIALS

1170 (1320, 1490, 1650, 1840, 2055) yards of chunky weight wool yarn

6 (7, 8, 9, 10, 11) skeins of Brooklyn Tweed *Quarry* (100% American Targhee-Columbia wool; 200 yards/100 grams)

Photographed in color *Geode*

GAUGE

14 stitches & 22 rows = 4" in stockinette stitch with Size A needle(s), after blocking

28-stitch panel from Cable Chart measures approximately 5¾" wide with Size A needle(s), after blocking

NEEDLES

Size A (for Main Fabric)

One pair of straight needles or a 32" circular needle* in size needed to obtain gauges listed

Suggested Size: 6½ mm (US 10½)

Size B (for Ribbing)

One pair of straight needles or a 32" circular needle*, one size smaller than Size A

Suggested Size: 6 mm (US 10)

Knitter's preferred style of needle may be used

Core strengthening. Supple cables firmly anchored at the centerline mark this quick-knitting pullover and a ribbed shawl collar provides double the woolen warmth.

ADDITIONAL TOOLS

Stitch markers, removable markers, stitch holders or waste yarn, cable needle (CN), blunt tapestry needle, T-pins (optional), a small amount of firmly spun yarn in a similar color for seaming (see *Construction Notes*)

FINISHED DIMENSIONS

34¼ (38¾, 43¼, 47¾, 52¾, 57¼)" [87 (98.5, 110, 121.5, 134, 145.5) cm] circumference at bust
Intended Ease: + 2–4" [5–10 cm]
Sample shown is size 38¾" [98.5 cm] with 4¾" [12 cm] ease on model

SKILL LEVEL

● ● ● ○ ○

CONSTRUCTION NOTES

The pieces are worked flat from the bottom up and sewn together. The collar is worked flat separately and sewn to the neck edge.

The Sloped Bind Off (see *Special Techniques*) is used when shaping the armholes, shoulders, and sleeve caps.

Read RS (odd-numbered) chart rows from right to left; read WS (even-numbered) chart rows from left to right.

The chart includes left and right cable crosses (LC and RC) where knit stitches are crossed over knit stitches and left and right cable twists (LT and RT) where knit stitches are crossed over purl stitches.

When working shaping, if there are not enough stitches to work a cable cross or twist, work the affected stitches in stockinette stitch.

Slip markers as they are encountered.

Where {knit 1} appears in braces, it indicates a selvedge stitch.

Because of the softly spun nature of *Quarry*, some knitters prefer to do their seaming with a firmly spun yarn in a similar color; alternatively, you may add twist into the yarn (in the same direction as the yarn is plied) as you seam to add tensile strength. When weaving in ends, twist the yarn several times in the same direction in which it is plied before threading the tapestry needle with the yarn end. Add more twist as you sew, if necessary. You may wish to weave in the ends as you go.

For more information on working with *Quarry*, see our Tip Card at www.brooklyntweed.com/tips/quarry.

BINGHAM

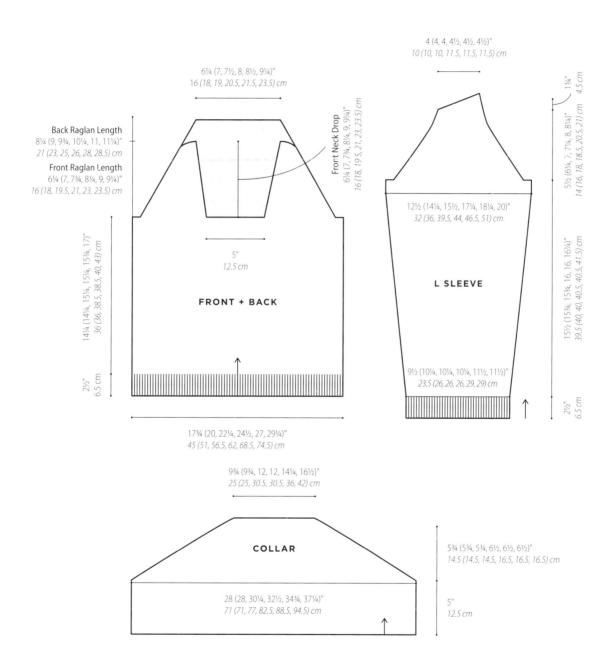

4 (4, 4, 4½, 4½, 4½)"
10 (10, 10, 11.5, 11.5, 11.5) cm

6¼ (7, 7½, 8, 8½, 9¼)"
16 (18, 19, 20.5, 21.5, 23.5) cm

Front Neck Drop
6¼ (7, 7¾, 8¼, 9, 9¼)"
16 (18, 19.5, 21, 23, 23.5) cm

1¾"
4.5 cm

Back Raglan Length
8¼ (9, 9¾, 10¼, 11, 11¼)"
21 (23, 25, 26, 28, 28.5) cm

Front Raglan Length
6¼ (7, 7¾, 8¼, 9, 9¼)"
16 (18, 19.5, 21, 23, 23.5) cm

5½ (6¼, 7, 7¼, 8, 8¼)"
14 (16, 18, 18.5, 20.5, 21) cm

5"
12.5 cm

14¼ (14¼, 15¼, 15¼, 15¾, 17)"
36 (36, 38.5, 38.5, 40, 43) cm

FRONT + BACK

12½ (14¼, 15½, 17¼, 18¼, 20)"
32 (36, 39.5, 44, 46.5, 51) cm

L SLEEVE

15½ (15¾, 15¾, 16, 16, 16¼)"
39.5 (40, 40, 40.5, 40.5, 41.5) cm

2½"
6.5 cm

9½ (10¼, 10¼, 10¼, 11½, 11½)"
23.5 (26, 26, 26, 29, 29) cm

2½"
6.5 cm

17¾ (20, 22¼, 24½, 27, 29¼)"
45 (51, 56.5, 62, 68.5, 74.5) cm

9¾ (9¾, 12, 12, 14¼, 16½)"
25 (25, 30.5, 30.5, 36, 42) cm

COLLAR

5¾ (5¾, 5¾, 6½, 6½, 6½)"
14.5 (14.5, 14.5, 16.5, 16.5, 16.5) cm

5"
12.5 cm

28 (28, 30¼, 32½, 34¾, 37¼)"
71 (71, 77, 82.5, 88.5, 94.5) cm

STITCH PATTERN

2X2 RIBBING
Multiple of 4 stitches; 2-row repeat

Row 1 (RS): {Knit 1}, knit 2, *purl 2, knit 2; repeat from * to last stitch, {knit 1}.
Row 2 (WS): {Knit 1}, purl 2, *knit 2, purl 2; repeat from * to last stitch, {knit 1}.

Repeat Rows 1 & 2 for pattern.

BACK

With Size B needle(s) (suggested size: 6 mm/US 10), cast on 70 (78, 86, 94, 102, 110) stitches using your preferred method. Do not join; work back and forth in rows.

WORK RIBBING
Setup Row (WS): {Knit 1}, [purl 2, knit 2] 6 (7, 8, 9, 10, 11) times, purl 4, knit 2, purl 8, knit 2, purl 4, [knit 2, purl 2] 6 (7, 8, 9, 10, 11) times, {knit 1}.

Row 1 (RS): {Knit 1}, [knit 2, purl 2] 6 (7, 8, 9, 10, 11) times, knit 4, purl 2, knit 8, purl 2, knit 4, [purl 2, knit 2] 6 (7, 8, 9, 10, 11) times, {knit 1}.
Row 2 (WS): Repeat Setup Row.

Repeat Rows 1 & 2 five more times. Piece measures approximately 2½" from cast-on edge, ending with a WS row.

MAIN PATTERN
Switch to Size A needle(s) (suggested size: 6½ mm/US 10½).

Next Row (RS): {Knit 1}, knit 19 (23, 27, 31, 35, 39), purl 1, place marker, work Row 1 of Cable Chart over 28 stitches, place marker, purl 1, knit 19 (23, 27, 31, 35, 39), {knit 1}.

Next Row (WS): {Knit 1}, purl 19 (23, 27, 31, 35, 39), knit 1, slip marker, work Row 2 of Cable Chart to marker, slip marker, knit 1, purl 19 (23, 27, 31, 35, 39), {knit 1}.

Work even in established pattern until piece measures 16¾ (16¾, 17¾, 17¾, 18¼, 19½)" from cast-on edge ending with Row 6 or 8 of chart (make note of which row was worked last).

SHAPE RAGLAN ARMHOLES

Bind off 3 (4, 6, 7, 8, 10) stitches at the beginning of the next 2 rows. [64 (70, 74, 80, 86, 90) stitches remain]

Work 2 rows even in established pattern.

Raglan Decrease Row (RS): {Knit 1}, knit 2, k2tog, work as established to last 5 stitches, SSK, knit 2, {knit 1}. (2 stitches decreased)

Repeat the Raglan Decrease Row every 4th row 4 (4, 5, 4, 4, 4) more times, then every RS row 12 (14, 14, 17, 19, 20) times.

Upon completion of this section, you will have worked the Raglan Decrease Row a total of 17 (19, 20, 22, 24, 25) times; you now have 30 (32, 34, 36, 38, 40) stitches on your needle(s).

Work 1 row even in established pattern (WS).

Bind off all stitches in pattern, working according to Binding Off Over Cabled Fabrics (see *Special Techniques*) on center panel.

FRONT

Work as for back until piece measures 16¾ (16¾, 17¾, 17¾, 18¼, 19½)" from cast-on edge, ending with the same chart row on which you ended the back.

SHAPE NECK AND RAGLANS

Note: Neck and raglan shaping are worked at the same time. Please read the following section through to the end before proceeding.

Next Row (RS): Bind off 3 (4, 6, 7, 8, 10) stitches, work 20 (23, 25, 28, 31, 33) stitches as established (including last stitch from bind-off), join a new ball of yarn and bind off center 24 stitches according to Binding Off Over Cabled Fabrics, work as established to end. [20 (23, 25, 28, 31, 33) stitches remain for right front and 23 (27, 31, 35, 39, 43) stitches remain for left front]

Both sides will be worked at once from separate balls of yarn from this point forward. Make sure not to cross or twist yarns when switching to second side.

Next Row (WS): Bind off 3 (4, 6, 7, 8, 10) stitches, work as established to 1 stitch before neck edge, {knit 1}; on second side with other ball of yarn, {knit 1}, work as established to end. [20 (23, 25, 28, 31, 33) stitches remain on each side]

Neck Decrease Row (RS): Work as established to 4 stitches before neck edge, SSK, remove marker, knit 1, {knit 1}; on second side with other ball of yarn, {knit 1}, knit 1, remove marker, k2tog, work as established to end. (1 stitch decreased at each neck edge)

Repeat the Neck Decrease Row every 12th (10th, 8th, 6th, 6th, 6th) row 1 (3, 3, 2, 4, 7) more time(s), then every 14th (0, 10th, 8th, 8th, 0) row 1 (0, 1, 3, 2, 0) time(s) and, AT THE SAME TIME beginning with the following RS row after first Neck Decrease Row, shape raglans as follows:

Raglan Decrease Row (RS): {Knit 1}, knit 2, k2tog, work as established to neck edge; on second side with other ball of yarn, work as established to last 5 stitches, SSK, knit 2, {knit 1}. (2 stitches decreased)

Repeat the Raglan Decrease Row every 4th row 4 (4, 5, 4, 4, 4) more times, then every RS row 4 (6, 6, 9, 11, 12) times. [8 stitches remain on each side when all shaping is complete]

Note: Please review Sloped Bind Off (see Special Techniques) before proceeding.

Next Row (WS): Bind off 2 stitches, work as established to 1 stitch before neck edge, {knit 1}; on second side with other ball of yarn, {knit 1}, work as established to end.

Next Row (RS): Bind off 2 stitches, work as established to 1 stitch before neck edge, {knit 1}; on second side with other ball of yarn, {knit 1}, work as established to end. [6 stitches remain on each side]

Working in the same manner, bind off 3 stitches from each side once more. [3 stitches remain on each side]

Bind off remaining stitches on each side.

LEFT SLEEVE

With Size B needle(s), cast on 32 (36, 36, 36, 40, 40) stitches using your preferred method.

WORK RIBBING

Beginning and ending with a WS row, work 2x2 Ribbing (see *Stitch Pattern*) until piece measures 2½" from cast-on edge, ending with a WS row.

MAIN PATTERN

Switch to Size A needle(s).

Next Row (RS): {Knit 1}, knit to last stitch, {knit 1}.
Next Row (WS): {Knit 1}, purl to last stitch, {knit 1}.

SHAPE SLEEVE

Sleeve Increase Row (RS): {Knit 1}, knit 1, M1R, knit to last 2 stitches, M1L, knit 1, {knit 1}. (2 stitches increased)

Repeat the Sleeve Increase Row every 16th (12th, 10th, 8th, 8th, 6th) row 1 (6, 4, 4, 4, 10) more time(s), then every 14th (0, 8th, 6th, 6th, 4th) row 4 (0, 4, 7, 7, 4) times.

Upon completion of this section, you will have worked the Sleeve Increase Row a total of 6 (7, 9, 12, 12, 15) times; you now have 44 (50, 54, 60, 64, 70) stitches on your needle.

Work even until piece measures 18 (18¼, 18¼, 18½, 18½, 18¾)" from cast-on edge, ending with a WS row.

SHAPE RAGLAN CAP

Bind off 3 (4, 6, 7, 8, 10) stitches at the beginning of the next 2 rows. [38 (42, 42, 46, 48, 50) stitches remain]

Raglan Decrease Row (RS): {Knit 1}, knit 1, k2tog, knit to last 4 stitches, SSK, knit 1, {knit 1}. (2 stitches decreased)

Repeat the Raglan Decrease Row every RS row 9 (11, 9, 10, 10, 11) more time(s), then every 4th row 2 (2, 4, 4, 5, 5) times.

Upon completion of this section, you will have worked the Raglan Decrease Row a total of 12 (14, 14, 15, 16, 17) times; you now have 14 (14, 14, 16, 16, 16) stitches on your needle.

Work 1 WS row even.

SHAPE TOP

Use the Sloped Bind Off in this section for best results.

Work 1 RS row even.

Next Row (WS): Bind off 3 (3, 3, 4, 4, 4) stitches, work as established to end. [11 (11, 11, 12, 12, 12) stitches remain]

Next Row (RS): {Knit 1}, knit 1, k2tog, work as established to end. [10 (10, 10, 11, 11, 11) stitches remain]

At the beginning of WS rows, bind off 3 (3, 3, 4, 4, 4) stitches once, then bind off 3 stitches once, then bind off 2 stitches twice. [no stitches remain]

RIGHT SLEEVE

Work as for Left Sleeve to beginning of "Shape Top" section.

SHAPE TOP

Use the Sloped Bind Off in this section for best results.

Next Row (RS): Bind off 3 (3, 3, 4, 4, 4) stitches, work as established to end. [11 (11, 11, 12, 12, 12) stitches remain]

Work 1 row even (WS).

Next Row (RS): Bind off 3 (3, 3, 4, 4, 4) stitches, work as established to last 4 stitches, SSK, knit 1, {knit 1}. [7 stitches remain]

Work 1 row even (WS).

At the beginning of RS rows, bind off 3 stitches once, then bind off 2 stitches twice. [no stitches remain]

COLLAR

With Size B needle(s), cast on 98 (98, 106, 114, 122, 130) stitches using your preferred method.

Next Row (WS): {Knit 1}, purl 1, *knit 2, purl 2; repeat from * to last 4 stitches, knit 2, purl 1, {knit 1}.
Next Row (RS): {Knit 1}, knit 1, *purl 2, knit 2; repeat from * to last 4 stitches, purl 2, knit 1, {knit 1}.

Repeat the last 2 rows until piece measures 5" from cast-on edge, ending with a WS row.

Decrease Row 1 (RS): {Knit 1}, knit 1, k2tog (or p2tog to keep in pattern), work in established pattern to last 4 stitches, SSK (or SSP to keep in pattern), knit 1, {knit 1}. (2 stitches decreased)

Decrease Row 2 (WS): {Knit 1}, purl 1, SSP (or SSK to keep in pattern), work in established pattern to last 4 stitches, p2tog (or k2tog to keep in pattern), purl 1, {knit 1}. (2 stitches decreased)

Repeat the last 2 rows 15 (15, 15, 17, 17, 17) more times. [34 (34, 42, 42, 50, 58) stitches remain]

Bind off all stitches in pattern.

FINISHING

Wet-block pieces to schematic measurements (see *Special Techniques*). With matching firmly spun yarn threaded on a tapestry needle (see *Construction Notes*), sew raglan seams, taking care to place left and right sleeves correctly. Sew side and sleeve seams.

Sew bound-off/decreased edge of collar to neck edge such that the knit stitch adjacent to the selvedge stitch is on the RS and will line up next to the bound-off center front neck stitches. Sew side edges of collar to center front bound-off stitches, with right side lapped over left side.

Weave in any remaining ends invisibly on the WS of fabric (see *Construction Notes*). Fold collar back. Steam seams and collar or wet-block entire garment again.

BINGHAM

CHART

CABLE CHART

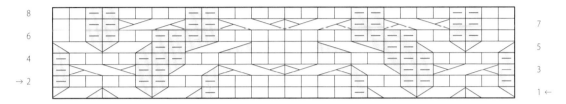

8

6

4

→ 2

7

5

3

1 ←

28-stitch panel
8-row repeat

	Knit
	Knit stitch on RS; purl stitch on WS

Knit
Knit stitch on RS; purl stitch on WS

Purl
Purl stitch on RS; knit stitch on WS

2/2 LC (Left Cross)
Slip 2 stitches to CN and hold in front, knit 2 stitches from
L needle, knit 2 stitches from CN

2/2 RC (Right Cross)
Slip 2 stitches to CN and hold in back, knit 2 stitches from
L needle, knit 2 stitches from CN

2/1 LT (Left Twist)
Slip 2 stitches to CN and hold in front, purl 1 stitch from
L needle, knit 2 stitches from CN

2/1 RT (Right Twist)
Slip 1 stitch to CN and hold in back, knit 2 stitches from
L needle, purl stitch from CN

2/2 LT
Slip 2 stitches to CN and hold in front, purl 2 stitches from
L needle, knit 2 stitches from CN

2/2 RT
Slip 2 stitches to CN and hold in back, knit 2 stitches from
L needle, purl 2 stitches from CN

95

CELYN

OVERVIEW

SCHEMATIC
98

PATTERN
99

CHARTS
105

MATERIALS

1520 (1615, 1880, 1990, 2265, 2400) yards of worsted weight wool yarn

11 (12, 14, 15, 17, 18) skeins of Brooklyn Tweed *Shelter* (100% American Targhee-Columbia wool; 140 yards/50 grams)

Photographed in color *Snowbound*

GAUGE

20 stitches & 30 rows = 4" in stockinette stitch with Size A needle(s), after blocking

26 stitches & 32 rows = 4" in chart pattern with Size A needle(s), after blocking

NEEDLES

Size A (for Main Fabric)
One 32" circular needle in size needed to obtain gauge listed
Suggested Size: 4½ mm (US 7)
Size B (for Ribbing)
One 40" circular needle, two sizes smaller than Size A
Suggested Size: 3¾ mm (US 5)

The interest is in the asymmetry. A cabled matrix tilts across the back of this cardigan to challenge the balance of the mirrored fronts.

ADDITIONAL TOOLS

Stitch markers, removable markers, stitch holders or waste yarn, cable needle (CN), T-pins (optional), blunt tapestry needle, 5 (5, 6, 6, 6, 6) 1" buttons, a small amount of sock yarn in a similar color for seaming (see *Construction Notes*)

FINISHED DIMENSIONS

36¼ (38½, 43¼, 46, 51, 53¼)" [92 (98, 110, 117, 129.5, 135.5) cm] circumference at bust, buttoned
Intended Ease: + 3–5" [7.5–12.5 cm]
Sample shown is size 38½" [98 cm] with 4½" [11.5 cm] ease on model

SKILL LEVEL

● ● ● ● ○

CONSTRUCTION NOTES

This cardigan is worked in pieces from the bottom up and sewn together. The button/buttonhole band is picked up around the front edges and back neck edge and worked flat.

Pieces are worked flat on a circular needle to accommodate the large number of stitches. A longer Size B needle is required due to the width of the collar.

The Sloped Bind Off (see *Special Techniques*) is used when shaping the armholes, shoulders, and sleeve caps.

Read RS (odd-numbered) chart rows from right to left; read WS (even-numbered) chart rows from left to right. Review the charts carefully as different charts are used for different pieces.

While working shaping or when a start/end point for your size intersects a cable, if you do not have enough stitches to complete the cable, work the affected stitches as knit or purl as they appear.

Where {knit 1} appears in braces, it indicates a selvedge stitch.

Because of the softly spun nature of *Shelter*, some knitters prefer to do their seaming with a firmly spun yarn, such as sock yarn, in a similar color; alternatively, you may add twist into the yarn (in the same direction as the yarn is plied) as you seam to add tensile strength.

CELYN

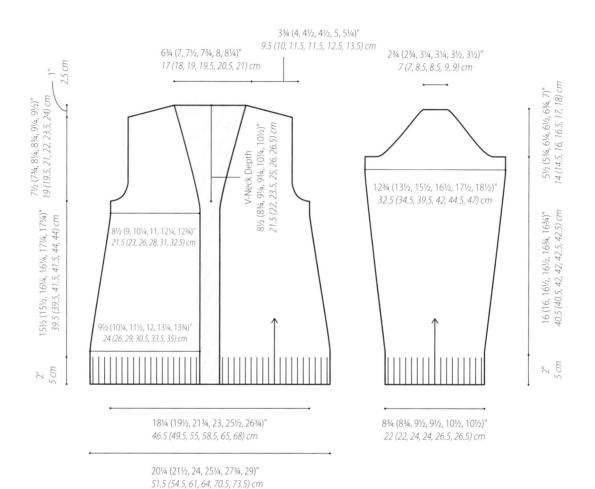

3¾ (4, 4½, 4½, 5, 5¼)"
9.5 (10, 11.5, 11.5, 12.5, 13.5) cm

6¾ (7, 7½, 7¾, 8, 8¼)"
17 (18, 19, 19.5, 20.5, 21) cm

2¾ (2¾, 3¼, 3¼, 3½, 3½)"
7 (7, 8.5, 8.5, 9, 9) cm

1"
2.5 cm

7½ (7¾, 8¼, 8¾, 9¼, 9½)"
19 (19.5, 21, 22, 23.5, 24) cm

V-Neck Depth
8½ (8¾, 9¼, 9¾, 10¼, 10½)"
21.5 (22, 23.5, 25, 26, 26.5) cm

5½ (5¾, 6¼, 6½, 6¾, 7)"
14 (14.5, 16, 16.5, 17, 18) cm

8½ (9, 10¼, 11, 12¼, 12¾)"
21.5 (23, 26, 28, 31, 32.5) cm

12¾ (13½, 15½, 16½, 17½, 18½)"
32.5 (34.5, 39.5, 42, 44.5, 47) cm

15½ (15½, 16¼, 16¼, 17¼, 17¼)"
39.5 (39.5, 41.5, 41.5, 44, 44) cm

16 (16, 16½, 16½, 16¾, 16¾)"
40.5 (40.5, 42, 42, 42.5, 42.5) cm

9½ (10¼, 11½, 12, 13¼, 13¾)"
24 (26, 29, 30.5, 33.5, 35) cm

2"
5 cm

2"
5 cm

18¼ (19½, 21¾, 23, 25½, 26¾)"
46.5 (49.5, 55, 58.5, 65, 68) cm

8¾ (8¾, 9½, 9½, 10½, 10½)"
22 (22, 24, 24, 26.5, 26.5) cm

20¼ (21½, 24, 25¼, 27¾, 29)"
51.5 (54.5, 61, 64, 70.5, 73.5) cm

CELYN

STITCH PATTERN

2X2 RIBBING
Multiple of 4 stitches; 2-row repeat

Row 1 (RS): {Knit 1}, knit 2, *purl 2, knit 2; repeat from * to last stitch, {knit 1}.
Row 2 (WS): {Knit 1}, purl 2, *knit 2, purl 2; repeat from * to last stitch, {knit 1}.

Repeat Rows 1 & 2 for pattern.

BACK

With Size B 40" circular needle (suggested size: 3¾ mm/ US 5) cast on 132 (140, 156, 164, 180, 188) stitches using your preferred method. Do not join; work back and forth in rows.

WORK RIBBING
Begin 2x2 Ribbing (see *Stitch Pattern*); work even until piece measures approximately 2" from cast-on edge, ending with a WS row.

BEGIN MAIN PATTERN
Switch to Size A 32" circular needle (suggested size: 4½ mm/US 7).

Next Row (RS): {Knit 1}, [knit 2, purl 2] twice, place marker, beginning and ending where indicated for back, work Row 1 of Chart A to last 9 stitches, place marker, [purl 2, knit 2] twice, {knit 1}.

Next Row (WS): {Knit 1}, [purl 2, knit 2] twice, slip marker, work Row 2 of Chart A to marker, slip marker, [knit 2, purl 2] twice, {knit 1}.

Work even in established pattern for 14 (14, 18, 18, 14, 14) more rows.

SHAPE SIDES
Side Decrease Row (RS): {Knit 1}, k2tog (or p2tog to keep in pattern), work as established to last 3 stitches, SSK (or SSP to keep in pattern), {knit 1}. (2 stitches decreased)

Repeat the Side Decrease Row every 16th (16th, 16th, 16th, 18th, 18th) row 6 more times.

Upon completion of this section you will have worked the Side Decrease Row a total of 7 times; you now have 118 (126, 142, 150, 166, 174) stitches on your needle.

Work even in established pattern until piece measures 17½ (17½, 18¼, 18¼, 19¼, 19¼)" from cast-on edge, ending with a WS row.

SHAPE ARMHOLES

Please review Sloped Bind Off and Binding Off Over Cabled Fabrics (see Special Techniques) before proceeding. Bind off in pattern.

Bind off 5 (6, 8, 9, 10, 11) stitches at the beginning of the next 2 rows, then bind off 4 stitches at the beginning of the next 2 rows, then bind off 2 stitches at the beginning of the next 2 (2, 2, 2, 4, 4) rows, then bind off 1 stitch at the beginning of the next 4 (4, 8, 10, 12, 14) rows. [92 (98, 106, 110, 118, 122) stitches remain]

Next Row (RS): {Knit 1}, work as established to last stitch, {knit 1}.

Work even as established until armholes measure 7½ (7¾, 8¼, 8¾, 9¼, 9½)", ending with a WS row.

SHAPE SHOULDERS

Use the Sloped Bind Off and work according to Binding Off Over Cabled Fabrics for best results. Bind off in pattern.

Bind off 6 (7, 7, 7, 8, 9) stitches at the beginning of the next 4 rows, then bind off 6 (6, 7, 8, 8, 8) stitches at the beginning of the next 2 rows, then bind off 6 (6, 8, 8, 9, 8) stitches at the beginning of the next 2 rows. [44 (46, 48, 50, 52, 54) stitches remain]

Bind off remaining stitches.

LEFT FRONT

With Size B 40" circular needle cast on 62 (66, 74, 78, 86, 90) stitches using your preferred method.

WORK RIBBING

Row 1 (RS): {Knit 1}, *knit 2, purl 2; repeat from * to last stitch, {knit 1}.
Row 2 (WS): Repeat Row 1.

Repeat the last 2 rows until piece measures 2" from cast-on edge, ending with a WS row.

BEGIN MAIN PATTERN

Switch to Size A 32" circular needle.

Next Row (RS): {Knit 1}, [knit 2, purl 2] twice, place marker, beginning and ending where indicated for your size, work Row 1 of Chart B to last 3 stitches, place marker, purl 2, {knit 1}.

Next Row (WS): {Knit 1}, knit 2, slip marker, work Row 2 of Chart B to marker, slip marker, [knit 2, purl 2] twice, {knit 1}.

Work even in established pattern for 14 (14, 18, 18, 14, 14) more rows.

SHAPE SIDE

Side Decrease Row (RS): {Knit 1}, k2tog (or p2tog to keep in pattern), work as established to last stitch, {knit 1}. (1 stitch decreased)

Repeat the Side Decrease Row every 16th (16th, 16th, 16th, 18th, 18th) row 6 more times.

Upon completion of this section you will have worked the Side Decrease Row a total of 7 times; you now have 55 (59, 67, 71, 79, 83) stitches on your needle.

Work even in established pattern until piece measures 17½ (17½, 18¼, 18¼, 19¼, 19¼)" from cast-on edge, ending with a WS row.

SHAPE ARMHOLE AND FRONT NECK

Note: Armhole and neck shaping are worked at the same time. Please read the following section through to the end before proceeding. Use the Sloped Bind Off and work according to Binding Off Over Cabled Fabrics for best results. Bind off in pattern and re-establish {knit 1} at armhole edge once bind-offs are complete.

Decrease Row (RS): Bind off 5 (6, 8, 9, 10, 11) stitches, work as established to last 4 stitches, SSK (or SSP to keep in pattern), knit 1, {knit 1}. [5 (6, 8, 9, 10, 11) stitches bound off at armhole edge; 1 stitch decreased at neck edge]

Next Row (WS): {Knit 1}, purl 1, work as established to end.

At the beginning of RS rows, bind off 4 stitches once, then bind off 2 stitches 1 (1, 1, 1, 2, 2) time(s), then bind off 1 stitch 2 (2, 4, 5, 6, 7) times and, AT THE SAME TIME, decrease 1 stitch at neck edge (as before) every RS row 8 (9, 9, 9, 10) more times, then every 4th row 9 (9, 10, 11, 12, 12) times.

Upon completion of this section you will have bound off a total of 13 (14, 18, 20, 24, 26) stitches at armhole edge and decreased a total of 18 (19, 20, 21, 22, 23) stitches at neck edge; you will have 24 (26, 29, 30, 33, 34) stitches on your needle when all shaping is complete.

Work even as established until armhole measures 7½ (7¾, 8¼, 8¾, 9¼, 9½)", ending with a WS row.

SHAPE SHOULDER

Use the Sloped Bind Off and work according to Binding Off Over Cabled Fabrics for best results. Bind off in pattern.

Bind off 6 (7, 7, 7, 8, 9) stitches at the beginning of the next 2 RS rows, then bind off 6 (6, 7, 8, 8, 8) stitches at the beginning of the next RS row. [6 (6, 8, 8, 9, 8) stitches remain]

Bind off remaining stitches on next RS row.

RIGHT FRONT

With Size B 40" circular needle cast on 62 (66, 74, 78, 86, 90) stitches using your preferred method.

WORK RIBBING
Row 1 (RS): {Knit 1}, *purl 2, knit 2; repeat from * to last stitch, {knit 1}.
Row 2 (WS): Repeat Row 1.

Repeat the last 2 rows until piece measures 2" from cast-on edge, ending with a WS row.

BEGIN MAIN PATTERN
Switch to Size A 32" circular needle.

Next Row (RS): {Knit 1}, purl 2, place marker, beginning and ending where indicated for right front for your size, work Row 1 of Chart A to last 9 stitches, place marker, [purl 2, knit 2] twice, {knit 1}.

Next Row (WS): {Knit 1}, [purl 2, knit 2] twice, slip marker, work Row 2 of Chart A to marker, slip marker, knit 2, {knit 1}.

Work even in established pattern for 14 (14, 18, 18, 14, 14) more rows.

SHAPE SIDE
Side Decrease Row (RS): {Knit 1}, work as established to last 3 stitches, SSK (or SSP to keep in pattern), {knit 1}. (1 stitch decreased)

Repeat the Side Decrease Row every 16th (16th, 16th, 16th, 18th, 18th) row 6 more times.

Upon completion of this section you will have worked the Side Decrease Row a total of 7 times; you now have 55 (59, 67, 71, 79, 83) stitches on your needle.

Work even in established pattern until piece measures 17½ (17½, 18¼, 18¼, 19¼, 19¼)" from cast-on edge, ending with a WS row.

SHAPE ARMHOLE AND FRONT NECK
Note: Armhole and neck shaping are worked at the same time. Please read the following section through to the end before proceeding. Use the Sloped Bind Off and work according to Binding Off Over Cabled Fabrics for best results. Bind off in pattern and re-establish {knit 1} at armhole edge once bind-offs are complete.

Decrease Row (RS): {Knit 1}, knit 1, k2tog (or p2tog to keep in pattern), work as established to end. (1 stitch decreased at neck edge)

Next Row (WS): Bind off 5 (6, 8, 9, 10, 11) stitches, work as established to last 2 stitches, purl 1, {knit 1}.

Decrease 1 stitch at neck edge (as before) every RS row 8 (9, 9, 9, 9, 10) more times, then every 4th row 9 (9, 10, 11, 12, 12) times and, AT THE SAME TIME at the beginning of WS rows, bind off 4 stitches once, then bind off 2 stitches 1 (1, 1, 1, 2, 2) time(s), then bind off 1 stitch 2 (2, 4, 5, 6, 7) times.

Upon completion of this section you will have bound off a total of 13 (14, 18, 20, 24, 26) stitches at armhole edge and decreased a total of 18 (19, 20, 21, 22, 23) stitches at neck edge; you will have 24 (26, 29, 30, 33, 34) stitches on your needle when all shaping is complete.

Work even as established until armhole measures 7½ (7¾, 8¼, 8¾, 9¼, 9½)", ending with a RS row.

SHAPE SHOULDER
Use the Sloped Bind Off and work according to Binding Off Over Cabled Fabrics for best results. Bind off in pattern.

Bind off 6 (7, 7, 7, 8, 9) stitches at the beginning of the next 2 WS rows, then bind off 6 (6, 7, 8, 8, 8) stitches at the beginning of the next WS row. [6 (6, 8, 8, 9, 8) stitches remain]

Bind off remaining stitches on next WS row.

SLEEVES (MAKE 2)

With Size B 40" circular needle cast on 44 (44, 48, 48, 52, 52) stitches using your preferred method.

WORK RIBBING
Begin 2x2 Ribbing; work even until piece measures approximately 2" from cast-on edge, ending with a WS row.

BEGIN MAIN PATTERN
Switch to Size A 32" circular needle.

Next Row (RS): {Knit 1}, knit to last stitch, {knit 1}.

Next Row (WS): {Knit 1}, purl to last stitch, {knit 1}.

Work even in established pattern for 6 more rows, ending with a WS row.

SHAPE SLEEVE
Sleeve Increase Row (RS): {Knit 1}, knit 2, M1R, knit to last 3 stitches, M1L, knit 2, {knit 1}. (2 stitches increased)

Repeat the Sleeve Increase Row every 12th (10th, 8th, 8th, 6th, 6th) row 3 (4, 8, 2, 17, 13) more times, then every 10th (8th, 6th, 6th, 0, 4th) row 6 (7, 6, 14, 0, 6) times.

Upon completion of this section, you will have worked the Sleeve Increase Row a total of 10 (12, 15, 17, 18, 20) times; you now have 64 (68, 78, 82, 88, 92) stitches on your needle.

Work even in established pattern until piece measures 18 (18, 18½, 18½, 18¾, 18¾)" from cast-on edge, ending with a WS row.

SHAPE SLEEVE CAP

Note: Use the Sloped Bind Off for best results.

Bind off 5 (6, 8, 9, 10, 11) stitches at the beginning of the next 2 rows, then bind off 0 (0, 2, 2, 2, 2) stitches at the beginning of the following 0 (0, 2, 2, 2, 2) rows. [54 (56, 58, 60, 64, 66) stitches remain]

Cap Decrease Row (RS): {Knit 1}, knit 2, k2tog, knit to last 5 stitches, SSK, knit 2, {knit 1}. (2 stitches decreased)

Repeat the Cap Decrease Row every RS row 19 (20, 20, 21, 22, 23) more times. [14 (14, 16, 16, 18, 18) stitches remain]

Work 1 row even (WS).

Bind off remaining stitches.

FINISHING

Wet-block pieces to schematic measurements (see *Special Techniques*). With matching sock yarn threaded on a tapestry needle (see *Construction Notes*) sew shoulder seams.

BUTTON/BUTTONHOLE BAND

With Size B 40" circular needle, RS facing, and beginning at bottom of right front, pick up and knit 155 (156, 165, 168, 178, 179) stitches up right front edge to shoulder seam, 40 (42, 44, 46, 46, 48) stitches along back neck, and 155 (156, 165, 168, 178, 179) stitches down left front edge, ending at bottom edge. [350 (354, 374, 382, 402, 406) stitches now on needle]

Next Row (WS): Slip 1 purlwise wyif, purl 1, *knit 2, purl 2; repeat from * to end.
Next Row (RS): Slip 1 purlwise wyib, knit 1, *purl 2, knit 2; repeat from * to end.

Work 3 more rows in established pattern, ending with a WS row.

Buttonhole Row (RS): Work 6 (6, 6, 6, 4, 4) stitches in rib, work 4-stitch One-Row Buttonhole (see *Special Techniques*), *work 20 (20, 16, 16, 18, 18) stitches in rib, work 4-stitch One-Row Buttonhole; repeat from * 3 (3, 4, 4, 4, 4) more times, work in rib to end.

Work 5 rows even as established, ending with a WS row.

Bind off all stitches in pattern.

Sew side and sleeve seams. Set in sleeves. Steam bands and seams gently or wet-block entire garment again. Sew on buttons to correspond to buttonholes.

CELYN

CHARTS

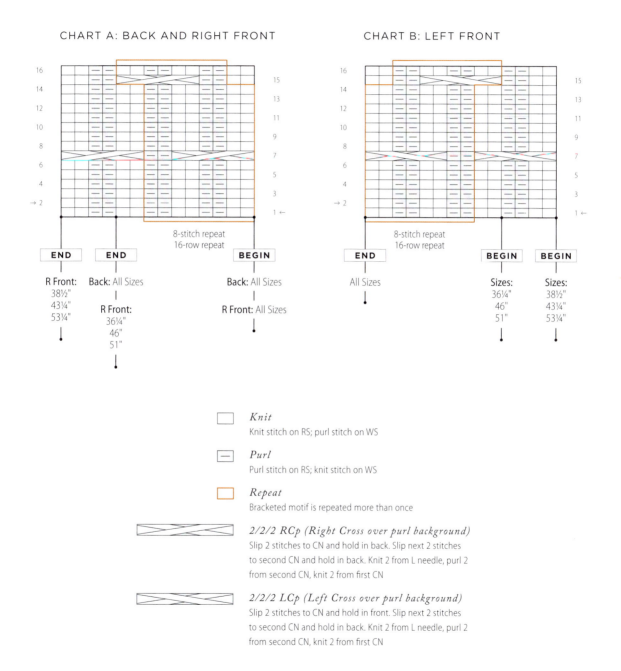

CHART A: BACK AND RIGHT FRONT

CHART B: LEFT FRONT

8-stitch repeat
16-row repeat

END
R Front:
38½"
43¼"
53¼"

END
Back: All Sizes
|
R Front:
36¼"
46"
51"

BEGIN
Back: All Sizes
|
R Front: All Sizes

END
All Sizes

BEGIN
Sizes:
36¼"
46"
51"

BEGIN
Sizes:
38½"
43¼"
53¼"

☐ *Knit*
Knit stitch on RS; purl stitch on WS

— *Purl*
Purl stitch on RS; knit stitch on WS

☐ *Repeat*
Bracketed motif is repeated more than once

2/2/2 RCp (Right Cross over purl background)
Slip 2 stitches to CN and hold in back. Slip next 2 stitches to second CN and hold in back. Knit 2 from L needle, purl 2 from second CN, knit 2 from first CN

2/2/2 LCp (Left Cross over purl background)
Slip 2 stitches to CN and hold in front. Slip next 2 stitches to second CN and hold in back. Knit 2 from L needle, purl 2 from second CN, knit 2 from first CN

CLERIDAE

OVERVIEW

SCHEMATIC
108

PATTERN
109

CHART
110

MATERIALS
195 yards of worsted weight wool yarn
2 skeins of Brooklyn Tweed *Shelter* (100% American Targhee-Columbia wool; 140 yards/50 grams)

Photographed in colors *Faded Quilt* & *Tent*

GAUGE
26 stitches & 32 rounds = 4" in chart pattern, after blocking

NEEDLES
One 16" circular needle and one set of double-pointed needles (DPNs)* in size needed to obtain gauge listed
Suggested Size: 4½ mm (US 7)
32" circular needle can be used instead of 16" circular and DPNs if using the Magic Loop method for working small circumferences in the round..

Reach up and stir the sky. The organic forms of bare branches and twisted trunks lend earthy beauty to this warm cap.

ADDITIONAL TOOLS

Stitch markers, cable needle (CN), 2" diameter pom-pom maker (optional; available at craft stores), blunt tapestry needle

FINISHED DIMENSIONS

17¼" [44 cm] circumference, unstretched (to comfortably fit average adult head sizes 20–22" [51–56 cm])
8¼" [21 cm] length

SKILL LEVEL

● ● ● ○ ○

CONSTRUCTION NOTES

The hat is worked in the round from the brim to the crown. An optional pom-pom may be added.

Read all chart rounds from right to left.

The chart includes left and right cable crosses (LC and RC) where knit stitches are crossed over knit stitches and left and right cable twists (LT and RT) where knit stitches are crossed over purl stitches.

CLERIDAE

SCHEMATIC

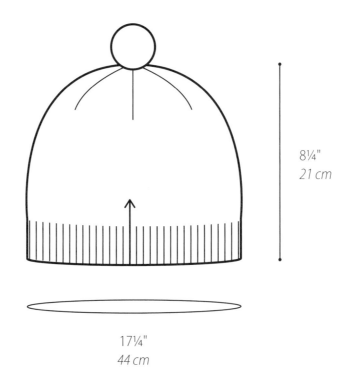

8¼"
21 cm

17¼"
44 cm

To fit average adult head sizes 20–22" [51–56 cm]

CLERIDAE

PATTERN

HAT

With 16" circular needle (suggested size: 4½ mm/US 7), cast on 112 stitches using your preferred method. Place marker for BOR and join for working in the round, being careful not to twist your ring of stitches.

BEGIN MAIN PATTERN

Work Rounds 1–42 of Hat Chart, working chart 8 times per round. Piece measures approximately 5¼" from cast-on edge.

Round 43: Remove BOR marker, knit 3, replace BOR marker, work in chart pattern to end.

Work Rounds 44–46.

Round 47: Remove BOR marker, purl 4, replace BOR marker, work in chart pattern to end.

Work Rounds 48–54. Piece measures approximately 6¾" from cast-on edge.

SHAPE CROWN

Note: Switch to DPNs when necessary for number of stitches in round.

Work Rounds 55–66 of chart, working decreases as charted. [32 stitches remain after Round 65]

Break yarn, leaving a 10" tail. Thread tail on a tapestry needle, add twist to the tail in the direction the yarn is plied to give it additional tensile strength, and then draw strand twice through remaining stitches. Pull gently to secure and fasten off on inside of hat.

FINISHING

Weave in remaining ends neatly on WS of hat. Wet-block hat to schematic measurements using flat method (see *Special Techniques*).

OPTIONAL POM-POM

With pom-pom maker, and working according to package instructions, create 2"-diameter pom-pom (or preferred size).

Alternatively, you can make your own pom-pom maker out of stiff cardboard. Draw a 3" diameter circle on the cardboard. Draw a second circle, 1" in diameter, centered inside the first. Draw a wedge, approximately 1" wide, joining the two circles. Cut out shape (will be shaped like a "C"). Cut out a second identical cardboard shape. Hold the two pieces of cardboard together and wind the yarn around them until the center hole is filled. With sharp scissors, cut the yarn around the perimeter of the cardboard shapes, then take a length of yarn and wrap it around the short cut strands, wrapping between the two cardboard shapes. Tie very tightly. Trim pom-pom evenly to 2" diameter. Sew pom-pom to top of hat.

CLERIDAE

CHART

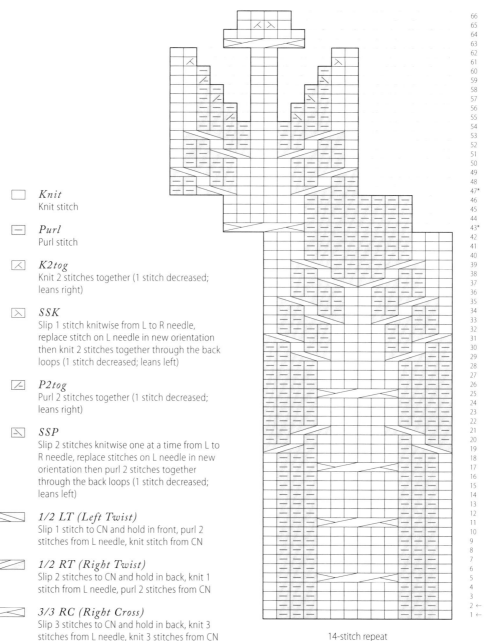

Knit
Knit stitch

Purl
Purl stitch

K2tog
Knit 2 stitches together (1 stitch decreased; leans right)

SSK
Slip 1 stitch knitwise from L to R needle, replace stitch on L needle in new orientation then knit 2 stitches together through the back loops (1 stitch decreased; leans left)

P2tog
Purl 2 stitches together (1 stitch decreased; leans right)

SSP
Slip 2 stitches knitwise one at a time from L to R needle, replace stitches on L needle in new orientation then purl 2 stitches together through the back loops (1 stitch decreased; leans left)

1/2 LT (Left Twist)
Slip 1 stitch to CN and hold in front, purl 2 stitches from L needle, knit stitch from CN

1/2 RT (Right Twist)
Slip 2 stitches to CN and hold in back, knit 1 stitch from L needle, purl 2 stitches from CN

3/3 RC (Right Cross)
Slip 3 stitches to CN and hold in back, knit 3 stitches from L needle, knit 3 stitches from CN

14-stitch repeat

See written pattern for special instructions for Rounds 43 & 47

110

ASPEN

OVERVIEW

MATERIALS

2485 (2675, 2975, 3220, 3550, 3765) yards of worsted weight wool yarn

18 (20, 22, 23, 26, 27) skeins of Brooklyn Tweed *Shelter* (100% American Targhee-Columbia wool; 140 yards/50 grams)

Photographed in color *Fossil*

GAUGE

25 stitches & 28 rows = 4" in chart patterns with Size A needle(s), after blocking

18 stitches & 28 rows = 4" in stockinette stitch with Size A needle(s), after blocking

NEEDLES

Size A (for Main Fabric)

One 32" circular needle in size needed to obtain gauge listed

Suggested Size: 5 mm (US 8)

Size B (for Ribbing, Pocket Linings, and Belt Loops)

One 47" circular needle and two double-pointed needles (DPNs), two sizes smaller than Size A

Suggested Size: 4 mm (US 6)

Pull out all the stops. Cables of soaring beauty deserve full expression, and there's no need to choose between coziness and elegance.

ADDITIONAL TOOLS

Stitch markers, locking markers or coilless safety pins, stitch holders or waste yarn, cable needle (CN), T-pins (optional), blunt tapestry needle, 8 (8, 8, 8, 9, 9) 1" buttons, a small amount of sock yarn in a similar color for seaming (see *Construction Notes*)

FINISHED DIMENSIONS

38 (41¼, 45¼, 49, 53¼, 57¼)" [96.5 (105, 115, 124.5, 135.5, 145.5) cm] circumference at bust, buttoned
Intended Ease: + 3–5" [7.5–12.5 cm]
Sample shown is size 41¼" [105 cm] with 7¼" [18.5 cm] ease on model

SKILL LEVEL

● ● ● ● ●

CONSTRUCTION NOTES

The cardigan is worked in pieces from the bottom up and sewn together. The collar stitches are picked up around the front edges and back neck edge. The collar is then worked flat and shaped using Short Rows: Turn & Slip Method (see *Special Techniques*).

The Sloped Bind Off (see *Special Techniques*) is used when shaping the armholes, shoulders, and sleeve caps.

Read RS (odd-numbered) chart rows from right to left; read WS (even-numbered) chart rows from left to right. Review the charts carefully as multiple charts are combined on each piece.

The chart includes left and right cable crosses (LC and RC) where knit stitches are crossed over knit stitches and left and right cable twists (LT and RT) where knit stitches are crossed over purl stitches.

While working shaping or when a start/end point for your size intersects a cable, if you do not have enough stitches to complete the cable, work the affected stitches as knit or purl as they appear.

Each size has a slightly different cable pattern setup at the side edges of the body.

Where {knit 1} appears in braces, it indicates a selvedge stitch.

Slip markers as you encounter them.

Pieces are worked flat on a circular needle to accommodate the large number of stitches. A longer Size B needle is required due to the width of the collar.

Because of the softly spun nature of *Shelter*, some knitters prefer to do their seaming with a firmly spun yarn, such as sock yarn, in a similar color; alternatively, you may add twist into the yarn (in the same direction as the yarn is plied) as you seam to add tensile strength.

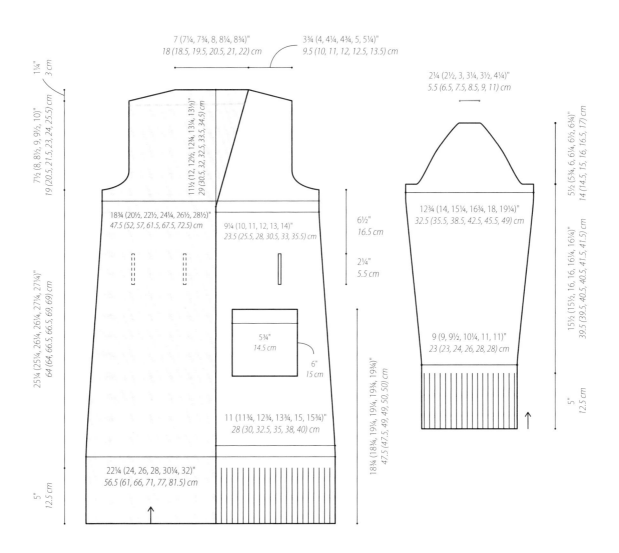

7 (7¼, 7¾, 8, 8¼, 8¾)"
18 (18.5, 19.5, 20.5, 21, 22) cm

3¾ (4, 4¼, 4¾, 5, 5¼)"
9.5 (10, 11, 12, 12.5, 13.5) cm

2¼ (2½, 3, 3¼, 3½, 4¼)"
5.5 (6.5, 7.5, 8.5, 9, 11) cm

1¼"
3 cm

7½ (8, 8½, 9, 9½, 10)"
19 (20.5, 21.5, 23, 24, 25.5) cm

11½ (12, 12½, 12¾, 13¼, 13½)"
29 (30.5, 32, 32.5, 33.5, 34.5) cm

5½ (5¾, 6, 6¼, 6½, 6¾)"
14 (14.5, 15, 16, 16.5, 17) cm

18¾ (20½, 22½, 24¼, 26½, 28½)"
47.5 (52, 57, 61.5, 67.5, 72.5) cm

9¼ (10, 11, 12, 13, 14)"
23.5 (25.5, 28, 30.5, 33, 35.5) cm

6½"
16.5 cm

12¾ (14, 15¼, 16¾, 18, 19¼)"
32.5 (35.5, 38.5, 42.5, 45.5, 49) cm

2¼"
5.5 cm

25¼ (25¼, 26¼, 26¼, 27¼, 27¼)"
64 (64, 66.5, 66.5, 69, 69) cm

15½ (15½, 16, 16, 16¼, 16¼)"
39.5 (39.5, 40.5, 40.5, 41.5, 41.5) cm

5¾"
14.5 cm

6"
15 cm

9 (9, 9½, 10¼, 11, 11)"
23 (23, 24, 26, 28, 28) cm

11 (11¾, 12¾, 13¾, 15, 15¾)"
28 (30, 32.5, 35, 38, 40) cm

18¾ (18¾, 19¼, 19¼, 19¾, 19¾)"
47.5 (47.5, 49, 49, 50, 50) cm

5"
12.5 cm

5"
12.5 cm

22¼ (24, 26, 28, 30¼, 32)"
56.5 (61, 66, 71, 77, 81.5) cm

5"
12.5 cm

ASPEN

PATTERN

STITCH PATTERN

2X2 RIBBING
Multiple of 4 stitches; 2-row repeat

Row 1 (RS): {Knit 1}, knit 2, *purl 2, knit 2; repeat from * to last stitch, {knit 1}.
Row 2 (WS): {Knit 1}, purl 2, *knit 2, purl 2; repeat from * to last stitch, {knit 1}.

Repeat Rows 1 & 2 for pattern.

POCKET LININGS (MAKE 2)

With Size B needle(s) (suggested size: 4 mm/US 6), cast on 36 stitches using your preferred method. Do not join.

Next Row (RS): {Knit 1}, knit to last stitch, {knit 1}.

Next Row (WS): {Knit 1}, purl to last stitch, {knit 1}.

Work even in established stockinette stitch with garter stitch selvedges until piece measures 6" from cast-on edge, ending with a WS row. Break yarn.

Transfer stitches to stitch holder or waste yarn.

Repeat instructions for second pocket lining.

BACK

With Size B 47" circular needle cast on 132 (144, 156, 168, 180, 192) stitches using your preferred method.

WORK RIBBING
Begin 2x2 Ribbing (see *Stitch Pattern*); work even until piece measures approximately 5" from cast-on edge, ending with a WS row.

BEGIN MAIN PATTERN
Switch to Size A 32" circular needle (suggested size: 5 mm/US 8).

Note: On the following row, begin with Row 1 of each chart. Please note that all charts are not worked for all sizes; take care to read the brackets carefully.

Next Row (RS): {Knit 1}, purl 11 (9, 10, 9, 12, 11), [place marker, work Right Rope Chart over 4 stitches, place marker, purl 1] 0 (0, 1, 1, 0, 0) time(s), [place marker, work Right Asymmetrical Braid Chart over 14 stitches, place marker, purl 1] 0 (0, 0, 0, 1, 1) time(s), [place marker, work Right Small Braid Chart over 6 stitches, place marker, purl 1] 1 (0, 0, 1, 0, 1) time(s), [place marker, work Right Asymmetrical Braid Chart over 14 stitches, place marker, purl 1] 0 (1, 1, 1, 1, 1) time(s), place marker, work Interlocking Chart over 36 stitches, place marker, purl 1, place marker, work Center Chart over 20 stitches, place marker, purl 1, place marker, work Interlocking Chart over 36 stitches, place marker, purl 1, [place marker, work Left Asymmetrical Braid Chart over 14 stitches, place marker, purl 1] 0 (1, 1, 1, 1, 1) time(s), [place marker, work Left Small Braid Chart over 6 stitches, place marker, purl 1] 1 (0, 0, 1, 0, 1) time(s), [place marker, work Left Asymmetrical Braid Chart over 14 stitches, place marker, purl 1] 0 (0, 0, 0, 1, 1) time(s), [place marker, work Left Rope Chart over 4 stitches, place marker, purl 1] 0 (0, 1, 1, 0, 0) time(s), purl 10 (8, 9, 8, 11, 10), {knit 1}.

Work even, working charts between markers as established, background stitches in reverse stockinette stitch (purl on RS; knit on WS), and each selvedge stitch in garter stitch (knit every row) until piece measures 7 (7, 8¼, 8¼, 7, 7)" from cast-on edge, ending with a WS row.

SHAPE SIDES AND PLACE BELT LOOP EYELETS

Note: Side shaping and belt loop eyelets are worked at the same time. Side shaping will begin first and will continue while belt loop eyelets are made. Please read the following section through to the end before proceeding.

Side Decrease Row (RS): {Knit 1}, p2tog, work as established to last 3 stitches, SSP, {knit 1}. (2 stitches decreased)

Repeat the Side Decrease Row every 20th (20th, 20th, 20th, 22nd, 22nd) row 7 more times and, AT THE SAME TIME when piece measures 21½ (21½, 22½, 22½, 23½, 23½)" from cast-on edge ending with a WS row, work eyelets over 2 rows as follows:

Eyelet Placement Row (RS): Work as established to 1 stitch before first Interlocking Chart, *slip marker, purl 1, YO, slip marker, work chart to marker; repeat from * 2 more times, slip marker, purl 1, YO, slip marker, work as established to end. (4 stitches increased)

Eyelet Decrease Row (WS): Work as established to 2 stitches before first Interlocking Chart, *slip marker, k2tog, slip marker, work chart to marker; repeat from * 2 more times, slip marker, k2tog, slip marker, work as established to end. (4 stitches decreased)

Work 14 rows in established pattern then repeat the Eyelet Placement Row and Eyelet Decrease Row once more. (4 pairs of eyelets worked, spaced 2¼" apart vertically)

Upon completion of this section you will have worked the Side Decrease Row a total of 8 times; you now have 116 (128, 140, 152, 164, 176) stitches on your needle.

Work even in established pattern until piece measures 30¼ (30¼, 31¼, 31¼, 32¼, 32¼)" from cast-on edge, ending with a WS row.

SHAPE ARMHOLES

Please review Sloped Bind Off and Binding Off Over Cabled Fabrics (see Special Techniques) before proceeding. Bind off in pattern.

Bind off 5 (6, 7, 8, 9, 10) stitches at the beginning of the next 2 rows, then bind off 4 stitches at the beginning of the next 2 rows, then bind off 2 (3, 3, 3, 3, 3) stitches at the beginning of the next 2 rows, then bind off 1 stitch at the beginning of the next 4 (6, 10, 14, 18, 22) rows. [90 (96, 102, 108, 114, 120) stitches remain]

Once bind-offs are complete, maintain pattern as follows beginning with next RS row:

For Size 38" Only: {Knit 1}, maintain pattern as much as possible over last 33 stitches of Interlocking chart, work center 22 stitches as established, maintain pattern as much as possible over first 33 stitches of Interlocking chart, {knit 1}.

For Size 41¼" Only: {Knit 1}, work charts as established over center 94 stitches, {knit 1}.

For Size 45¼" Only: {Knit 1}, purl 3, work charts as established over center 94 stitches, purl 3, {knit 1}.

For Size 49" Only: {Knit 1}, work 3 stitches as established, purl 3, work charts as established over center 94 stitches, purl 3, work 3 stitches as established, {knit 1}.

For Size 53¼" Only: Maintain pattern as established if necessary until Row 20 of Right and Left Asymmetrical Braid Charts is complete. Thereafter: {Knit 1}, work next 6 stitches as for Rows 5–8 of Right Asymmetrical Braid Chart, work 3 stitches in reverse stockinette stitch, work charts as established over center 94 stitches, work 3 stitches in reverse stockinette stitch, work next 6 stitches as for Rows 5–8 of Left Asymmetrical Braid Chart, {knit 1}.

For Size 57¼" Only: Maintain pattern as established if necessary until Row 20 of Right and Left Asymmetrical Braid Charts. Thereafter: {Knit 1}, work next 9 stitches as for Rows 1–8 of Right Asymmetrical Braid Chart, work 3 stitches in reverse stockinette stitch, work charts as established over center 94 stitches, work 3 stitches in reverse stockinette stitch, work next 9 stitches as for Rows 1–8 of Left Asymmetrical Braid Chart, {knit 1}.

Work even as established until armholes measure 7½ (8, 8½, 9, 9½, 10)", ending with a WS row.

SHAPE SHOULDERS
Use the Sloped Bind Off and work according to Binding Off Over Cabled Fabrics for best results. Bind off in pattern.

Bind off 6 (6, 7, 7, 8, 8) stitches at the beginning of the next 6 rows, then bind off 5 (7, 6, 8, 7, 9) stitches at the beginning of the next 2 rows. [44 (46, 48, 50, 52, 54) stitches remain]

Bind off remaining stitches.

LEFT FRONT

With Size B 47" circular needle cast on 62 (68, 74, 80, 86, 92) stitches using your preferred method.

WORK RIBBING
Begin 2x2 Ribbing; work even until piece measures approximately 5" from cast-on edge, ending with a WS row.

BEGIN MAIN PATTERN
Switch to Size A 32" circular needle.

Note: On the following row, begin with Row 1 of each chart. Please note that all charts are not worked for all sizes; take care to read the brackets carefully.

Next Row (RS): {Knit 1}, purl 11 (9, 10, 9, 12, 11), [place marker, work Right Rope Chart over 4 stitches, place marker, purl 1] 0 (0, 1, 1, 0, 0) time(s), [place marker, work Right Asymmetrical Braid Chart over 14 stitches, place marker, purl 1] 0 (0, 0, 0, 1, 1) time(s), [place marker, work Right Small Braid Chart over 6 stitches, place marker, purl 1] 1 (0, 0, 1, 0, 1) time(s), [place marker, work Right Asymmetrical Braid Chart over 14 stitches, place marker, purl 1] 0 (1, 1, 1, 1, 1) time(s), place marker, work Interlocking Chart over 36 stitches, place marker, purl 6, {knit 1}.

Work even, working charts between markers as established, background stitches in reverse stockinette stitch (purl on RS; knit on WS), and each selvedge stitch in garter stitch (knit every row) until piece measures 7 (7, 8¼, 8¼, 7, 7)" from cast-on edge, ending with a WS row.

SHAPE SIDE, PLACE POCKET, AND PLACE BELT LOOP EYELETS

Note: Side shaping, pocket placement, and belt loop eyelets are worked at the same time. Side shaping will begin first and will continue while pocket is placed and belt loop eyelets are made. Please read the following section through to the end before proceeding.

Side Decrease Row (RS): {Knit 1}, p2tog, work as established to end. (1 stitch decreased)

Repeat the Side Decrease Row every 20th (20th, 20th, 20th, 22nd, 22nd) row 7 more times and, AT THE SAME TIME when piece measures 18¾ (18¾, 19¼, 19¼, 19¾, 19¾)" from cast-on edge ending with a WS row, place pocket as follows:

Pocket Placement Row (RS): {Knit 1}, work as established to last 43 stitches, slip marker, transfer next 36 stitches to stitch holder or waste yarn for pocket, with RS facing transfer 36 held pocket lining stitches to L needle then work across them in chart pattern, slip marker, purl to last stitch, {knit 1}.

ALSO AT THE SAME TIME when piece measures 21½ (21½, 22½, 22½, 23½, 23½)" from cast-on edge ending with a WS row, work eyelet over 2 rows as follows:

Eyelet Placement Row (RS): Work as established to 1 stitch before Interlocking Chart, *slip marker, purl 1, YO, slip marker, work as established to end. (1 stitch increased)

Eyelet Decrease Row (WS): Work as established to end of Interlocking Chart, *slip marker, k2tog, slip marker, work as established to end. (1 stitch decreased)

Work 14 rows in established pattern then repeat the Eyelet Placement Row and Eyelet Decrease Row once more. (1 pair of eyelets worked, spaced 2¼" apart vertically)

Upon completion of this section you will have worked the Side Decrease Row a total of 8 times; you now have 54 (60, 66, 72, 78, 84) stitches on your needle.

Work even in established pattern until piece measures 27½ (27½, 28½, 28¾, 29¾, 30)" from cast-on edge, ending with a WS row.

SHAPE NECK AND ARMHOLE

Note: Neck and armhole shaping are worked at the same time. Neck shaping will begin first and will continue through armhole shaping. Please read the following section through to the end before proceeding. Please review Sloped Bind Off and Binding Off Over Cabled Fabrics before proceeding. Bind off in pattern.

Neck Decrease Row (RS): Work as established to last 3 stitches, SSP (or SSK to keep in pattern), {knit 1}. (1 stitch decreased)

Repeat the Neck Decrease Row every RS row 0 (0, 0, 1, 2, 3) more time(s), then every 4th row 17 (18, 19, 19, 19, 19) times and, AT THE SAME TIME when piece measures 30¼ (30¼, 31¼, 31¼, 32¼, 32¼)" from cast-on edge ending with a WS row, shape armhole as follows:

At the beginning of RS rows, bind off 5 (6, 7, 8, 9, 10) stitches once, then bind off 4 stitches once, then bind off 2 (3, 3, 3, 3, 3) stitches once, then bind off 1 stitch 2 (3, 5, 7, 9, 11) times. Maintain pattern as established over remaining stitches, working stitches near the armhole edge the same as you did for the back.

Upon completion of this section you will have bound off a total of 13 (16, 19, 22, 25, 28) stitches at armhole edge and decreased a total of 18 (19, 20, 21, 22, 23) stitches at neck edge; you will have 23 (25, 27, 29, 31, 33) stitches on your needle when all shaping is complete.

Work even as established until armhole measures 7½ (8, 8½, 9, 9½, 10)", ending with a WS row.

SHAPE SHOULDER

Use the Sloped Bind Off and work according to Binding Off Over Cabled Fabrics for best results. Bind off in pattern.

Bind off 6 (6, 7, 7, 8, 8) stitches at the beginning of the next 3 RS rows. [5 (7, 6, 8, 7, 9) stitches remain]

Bind off remaining stitches on next RS row.

RIGHT FRONT

With Size B 47" circular needle cast on 62 (68, 74, 80, 86, 92) stitches using your preferred method.

WORK RIBBING

Begin 2x2 Ribbing; work even until piece measures approximately 5" from cast-on edge, ending with a WS row.

BEGIN MAIN PATTERN

Switch to Size A 32" circular needle.

Note: On the following row, begin with Row 1 of each chart. Please note that all charts are not worked for all sizes; take care to read the brackets carefully.

Next Row (RS): {Knit 1}, purl 6, place marker, work Interlocking Chart over 36 stitches, place marker, purl 1, [place marker, work Left Asymmetrical Braid Chart over 14 stitches, place marker, purl 1] 0 (1, 1, 1, 1, 1) time(s), [place marker, work Left Small Braid Chart over 6 stitches, place marker, purl 1] 1 (0, 0, 1, 0, 1) time(s), [place marker, work Left Asymmetrical Braid Chart over 14 stitches, place marker, purl 1] 0 (0, 0, 0, 1, 1) time(s), [place marker, work

Left Rope Chart over 4 stitches, place marker, purl 1] 0 (0, 1, 1, 0, 0) time(s), purl 10 (8, 9, 8, 11, 10), {knit 1}.

Work even, working charts between markers as established, background stitches in reverse stockinette stitch (purl on RS; knit on WS), and each selvedge stitch in garter stitch (knit every row) until piece measures 7 (7, 8¼, 8¼, 7, 7)" from cast-on edge, ending with a WS row.

SHAPE SIDE, PLACE POCKET, AND PLACE BELT LOOP EYELETS

Note: Side shaping, pocket placement, and belt loop eyelets are worked at the same time. Side shaping will begin first and will continue while pocket is placed and belt loop eyelets are made. Please read the following section through to the end before proceeding.

Side Decrease Row (RS): Work as established to last 3 stitches, SSP, {knit 1}. (1 stitch decreased)

Repeat the Side Decrease Row every 20th (20th, 20th, 20th, 22nd, 22nd) row 7 more times and, AT THE SAME TIME when piece measures 18¾ (18¾, 19¼, 19¼, 19¾, 19¾)" from cast-on edge ending with a WS row, place pocket as follows:

Pocket Placement Row (RS): {Knit 1}, purl 6, slip marker, transfer next 36 stitches to stitch holder or waste yarn for pocket, with RS facing transfer 36 held pocket lining stitches to L needle then work across them in chart pattern, slip marker, work as established to end.

ALSO AT THE SAME TIME when piece measures 21½ (21½, 22½, 22½, 23½, 23½)" from cast-on edge ending with a WS row, work eyelet over 2 rows as follows:

Eyelet Placement Row (RS): Work as established to end of Interlocking Chart, *slip marker, purl 1, YO, slip marker, work as established to end. (1 stitch increased)

Eyelet Decrease Row (WS): Work as established to 2 stitches before Interlocking Chart, *slip marker, k2tog, slip marker, work as established to end. (1 stitch decreased)

Work 14 rows in established pattern then repeat the Eyelet Placement Row and Eyelet Decrease Row once more. (1 pair of eyelets worked, spaced 2¼" apart vertically)

Upon completion of this section you will have worked the Side Decrease Row a total of 8 times; you now have 54 (60, 66, 72, 78, 84) stitches on your needle.

Work even in established pattern until piece measures 27½ (27½, 28½, 28¾, 29¾, 30)" from cast-on edge, ending with a WS row.

SHAPE NECK AND ARMHOLE

Note: Neck and armhole shaping are worked at the same time. Neck shaping will begin first and will continue through armhole shaping. Please read the following section through to the end before proceeding. Please review Sloped Bind Off and Binding Off Over Cabled Fabrics before proceeding. Bind off in pattern.

Neck Decrease Row (RS): {Knit 1}, p2tog (or k2tog to keep in pattern), work as established to end. (1 stitch decreased)

Repeat the Neck Decrease Row every RS row 0 (0, 0, 1, 2, 3) more time(s), then every 4th row 17 (18, 19, 19, 19, 19) times and, AT THE SAME TIME when piece measures 30¼ (30¼, 31¼, 31¼, 32¼, 32¼)" from cast-on edge ending with a RS row, shape armhole as follows:

At the beginning of WS rows, bind off 5 (6, 7, 8, 9, 10) stitches once, then bind off 4 stitches once, then bind off 2 (3, 3, 3, 3, 3) stitches once, then bind off 1 stitch 2 (3, 5, 7, 9, 11) times. Maintain pattern as established over remaining stitches, working stitches near the armhole edge the same as you did for the back.

Upon completion of this section you will have bound off a total of 13 (16, 19, 22, 25, 28) stitches at armhole edge and decreased a total of 18 (19, 20, 21, 22, 23) stitches at neck edge; you will have 23 (25, 27, 29, 31, 33) stitches on your needle when all shaping is complete.

Work even as established until armhole measures 7½ (8, 8½, 9, 9½, 10)", ending with a RS row.

SHAPE SHOULDER
Use the Sloped Bind Off and work according to Binding Off Over Cabled Fabrics for best results. Bind off in pattern.

Bind off 6 (6, 7, 7, 8, 8) stitches at the beginning of the next 3 WS rows. [5 (7, 6, 8, 7, 9) stitches remain]

Bind off remaining stitches on next WS row.

SLEEVES (MAKE 2)

With Size B 47" circular needle cast on 56 (56, 60, 64, 68, 68) stitches using your preferred method.

WORK RIBBING
Begin 2x2 Ribbing; work even until piece measures approximately 5" from cast-on edge, ending with a WS row.

BEGIN MAIN PATTERN
Switch to Size A 32" circular needle.

Note: On the following row, begin with Row 1 of each chart.

Next Row (RS): {Knit 1}, beginning where indicated for your size, work Right Side Sleeve Chart over 15 (15, 17, 19, 21, 21) stitches, place marker, purl 2, place marker, work Center Chart over 20 stitches, place marker, purl 2, place marker, work Left Side Sleeve Chart over 15 (15, 17, 19, 21, 21) stitches ending where indicated for your size, {knit 1}. Work even in established pattern for 3 more rows, ending with a WS row.

SHAPE SLEEVE
Sleeve Increase Row (RS): {Knit 1}, M1R (or M1P to keep in pattern), work as established to last stitch, M1L (or M1P to keep in pattern), {knit 1}. (2 stitches increased)

Repeat the Sleeve Increase Row every 10th (6th, 6th, 6th, 6th, 4th) row 1 (15, 13, 9, 6, 23) more time(s), then every 8th (0, 4th, 4th, 4th, 2nd) row 10 (0, 4, 10, 15, 2) times, working new stitches into Right and Left Side Sleeve Chart patterns.

Upon completion of this section, you will have worked the Sleeve Increase Row a total of 12 (16, 18, 20, 22, 26) times; you now have 80 (88, 96, 104, 112, 120) stitches on your needle.

Work even in established pattern until piece measures 20½ (20½, 21, 21, 21¼, 21¼)" from cast-on edge, ending with a WS row.

SHAPE SLEEVE CAP

Use the Sloped Bind Off and work according to Binding Off Over Cabled Fabrics for best results. Bind off in pattern.

Bind off 5 (6, 7, 8, 9, 10) stitches at the beginning of the next 2 rows, then bind off 4 (5, 6, 6, 6, 6) stitches at the beginning of the following 2 rows, then bind off 3 stitches at the beginning of the next 2 rows, then bind off 2 stitches at the beginning of the following 2 (2, 2, 4, 4, 4) rows. [52 (56, 60, 62, 68, 74) stitches remain]

Bind off 1 stitch at the beginning of the next 26 (28, 30, 30, 30, 32) rows, then bind off 2 stitches at the beginning of the following 2 (2, 2, 2, 4, 4) rows, then bind off 4 stitches at the beginning of the next 2 rows. [14 (16, 18, 20, 22, 26) stitches remain]

Bind off remaining stitches.

FINISHING

Wet-block pieces to schematic measurements (see *Special Techniques*). With matching sock yarn threaded on a tapestry needle, sew shoulder seams (see *Construction Notes*).

COLLAR

With Size B 47" circular needle, RS facing, and beginning at bottom of right front, pick up and knit 142 (142, 150, 150, 158, 158) stitches up right front edge to first neck decrease, place marker, 65 (68, 73, 74, 77, 78) stitches up right neck edge to shoulder seam, 44 (46, 48, 50, 52, 54) stitches along back neck, 65 (68, 73, 74, 77, 78) stitches down left neck edge to first neck decrease, place marker, and 142 (142, 150, 150, 158, 158) stitches down left front edge ending at bottom edge. [458 (466, 494, 498, 522, 526) stitches now on needle]

Next Row (WS): Slip 1 purlwise wyif, purl 1, *knit 2, purl 2; repeat from * to end.

Note: Please Review Short Rows: Turn & Slip Method (see Special Techniques) before proceeding.

Short Row 1 (RS): Slip 1 purlwise wyib, [work in established rib pattern to marker, slip marker] twice, work 1 stitch in rib, turn & slip;
Short Row 2 (WS): Slip marker, work in established rib pattern to marker, slip marker, work 1 stitch in rib, turn & slip;

Short Row 3: Work in established rib pattern to 5 (5, 6, 6, 6, 7) stitches before gap from previous RS row, turn & slip;
Short Row 4: Work in established rib pattern to 5 (5, 6, 6, 6, 7) stitches before gap from previous WS row, turn & slip;

Short Rows 5–20: Repeat Short Rows 3 & 4 eight more times.

Next Row (RS): Work in established rib pattern to end, closing gaps as you go as described in *Special Techniques*.
Next Row (WS): Work in established rib pattern to end, closing remaining gaps as you go.

Work 2 rows even in established rib pattern, ending with a WS row.

Buttonhole Row (RS): Work 8 stitches in rib, work 4-stitch One-Row Buttonhole (see *Special Techniques*), *work 14 (14, 15, 15, 14, 14) stitches in rib, work 4-stitch One-Row Buttonhole; repeat from * 6 (6, 6, 6, 7, 7) more times, work in rib to end.

Work 1 row even (WS).

Repeat Short Rows 1–20 once more.

Next Row (RS): Work in established rib pattern to end, closing gaps as you go.
Next Row (WS): Work in established rib pattern to end, closing remaining gaps as you go.

Work even in established rib for 4 more rows, ending with a WS row.

Bind off all stitches in pattern.

BELT

With Size B DPNs cast on 12 stitches using your preferred method.

WORK RIBBING

Row 1 (RS): Slip 1 purlwise through the back loop wyif, knit 2, [purl 2, knit 2] twice, knit 1.
Row 2 (WS): Slip 1 knitwise wyib, purl 2, [knit 2, purl 2] twice, purl 1.

Repeat the last 2 rows until piece measures approximately 56¼ (60, 63¾, 67¾, 71½, 75¼)", ending with a WS row.

Bind off all stitches in pattern.

BELT LOOPS (MAKE 6)

With Size B DPNs, cast on 3 stitches using your preferred method.

Work I-Cord: *Slide stitches to opposite end of needle, pull yarn across back of work and knit 3; repeat from * until cord measures 4½" from beginning. Pull gently on cord periodically to neaten the work.

Break yarn leaving an 8" tail.

Thread yarn tail through 3 live stitches and pull snugly to fasten off.

Place Belt Loop: With WS facing, push cast-on end of I-cord through lower eyelet of any vertical pair of eyelets on garment body, from WS to RS. Turn work so that RS is facing, then push cast-on edge of I-cord through upper eyelet of pair from RS to WS.

Cast-on and bound-off edges of I-cord are now both on WS of garment. Using a tapestry needle and yarn tail (or a length of matching sock yarn), sew beginning and end of I-cord together to create a closed loop. Weave ends into center of I-cord.

Attach remaining belt loops to garment in the same fashion.

POCKET EDGINGS (MAKE 2)

Transfer held 36 pocket stitches to Size B needle(s). Rejoin yarn ready to work a RS row.

Begin 2x2 Ribbing; work even until edging measures 1".

Bind off all stitches in pattern.

Repeat instructions for second pocket edging.

Sew side edges of pocket edgings to RS of fronts. Sew sides and bottom of pocket linings to WS of fronts. Sew side and sleeve seams. Set in sleeves. Weave in ends. Steam collar and seams gently or wet-block entire garment again. Sew on buttons to correspond to buttonholes.

ASPEN

CHARTS

CENTER CHART

20-stitch panel
36-row repeat

LEFT SMALL BRAID CHART

6-stitch panel
4-row repeat

RIGHT SMALL BRAID CHART

6-stitch panel
4-row repeat

LEFT ROPE CHART

4-stitch panel
4-row repeat

RIGHT ROPE CHART

4-stitch panel
4-row repeat

☐ *Knit*
Knit stitch on RS; purl stitch on WS

⊟ *Purl*
Purl stitch on RS; knit stitch on WS

2/1 LT (Left Twist)
Slip 2 stitches to CN and hold in front, purl 1 stitch from L needle, knit 2 stitches from CN

2/1 RT (Right Twist)
Slip 1 stitch to CN and hold in back, knit 2 stitches from L needle, purl stitch from CN

2/2 LT
Slip 2 stitches to CN and hold in front, purl 2 stitches from L needle, knit 2 stitches from CN

2/2 RT
Slip 2 stitches to CN and hold in back, knit 2 stitches from L needle, purl 2 stitches from CN

2/2 LC (Left Cross)
Slip 2 stitches to CN and hold in front, knit 2 stitches from L needle, knit 2 stitches from CN

2/2 RC (Right Cross)
Slip 2 stitches to CN and hold in back, knit 2 stitches from L needle, knit 2 stitches from CN

ASPEN

CHARTS

RIGHT ASYMMETRICAL BRAID CHART

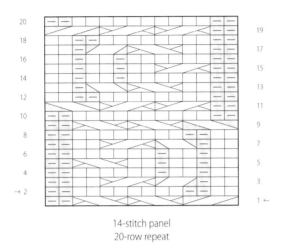

14-stitch panel
20-row repeat

LEFT ASYMMETRICAL BRAID CHART

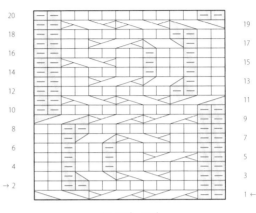

14-stitch panel
20-row repeat

INTERLOCKING CHART

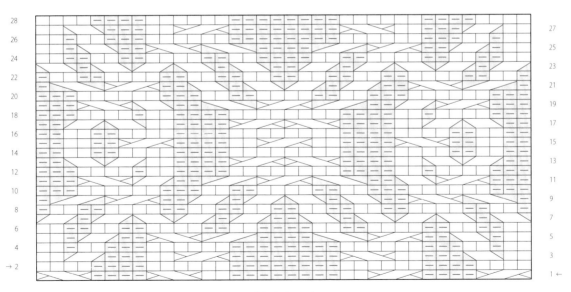

36-stitch panel
28-row repeat

ASPEN

CHARTS

RIGHT SIDE SLEEVE CHART

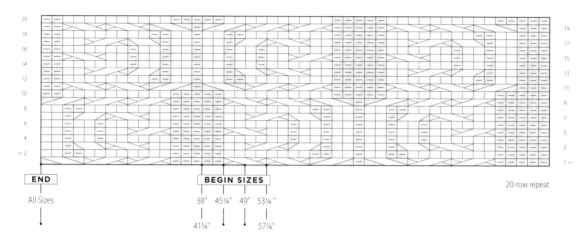

END

All Sizes

BEGIN SIZES

38"   45¼"   49"   53¼"

41¼"   57¼"

20-row repeat

LEFT SIDE SLEEVE CHART

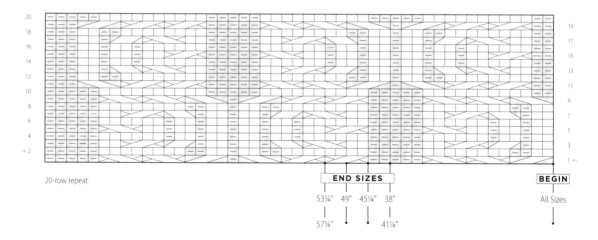

20-row repeat

END SIZES

53¼"   49"   45¼"   38"

57¼"   41¼"

BEGIN

All Sizes

126

GLOSSARY

|

129

GLOSSARY

ABBREVIATIONS

See Chart Legends for abbreviations not listed here.

BOR	Beginning of Round
CN	Cable Needle
DPN	Double-Pointed Needle
FD2-L	Fashioned Decrease Left – Double Place next 2 stitches onto CN and hold CN parallel to and in front of L needle. *Insert R needle into first stitch on CN and first stitch on L needle, knit these 2 stitches together; repeat from * once. (2 stitches decreased; leans left)
FD2-R	Fashioned Decrease Right – Double Place next 2 stitches onto CN and hold CN parallel to and behind L needle. *Insert R needle into first stitch on L needle and first stitch on CN, knit these 2 stitches together; repeat from * once. (2 stitches decreased; leans right)
K2TOG	Knit 2 Together Knit 2 stitches on L needle together. (1 stitch decreased; leans right)
L	Left Generally used in technique instructions to indicate which of your two working needles is being used

M1L Make 1 Left
With L needle tip, pick up the running thread between stitch just worked (below first stitch on R needle) and first stitch on L needle from front to back. Knit the running thread through the back loop. (1 stitch increased; leans left)

M1P Make 1 Purl
With L needle tip, pick up the running thread between stitch just worked (below first stitch on R needle) and first stitch on L needle from back to front. Purl the running thread through the front loop. (1 stitch increased)

M1R Make 1 Right
With L needle tip, pick up the running thread between stitch just worked (below first stitch on R needle) and first stitch on L needle from back to front. Knit the running thread through the front loop. (1 stitch increased; leans right)

P2TOG Purl 2 Together
Purl 2 stitches on L needle together.
(1 stitch decreased; leans right)

R Right
Generally used in technique instructions to indicate which of your two working needles is being used

RS Right Side
This term refers to the public side of the knitted fabric, i.e. the fabric that will be visible when garment is worn. In projects with reversible fabrics, RS will be assigned specifically at the beginning of the pattern.

SSK Slip, Slip, Knit (Modified)
Slip 1 stitch from L to R needle as if to knit, replace stitch on L needle in new orientation and knit 2 stitches from L needle together through the back loops. (1 stitch decreased; leans left)

SSP Slip, Slip, Purl
Slip 2 stitches knitwise, one at a time, transfer stitches back to L needle in their new orientation, then purl the stitches together through the back loops. (1 stitch decreased; leans left)

WS Wrong Side
This term refers to the non-public side of the knitted fabric, i.e. the fabric that will not be visible when garment is worn. In projects with reversible fabrics, WS will be assigned specifically at the beginning of the pattern.

WYIB With Yarn in Back

WYIF With Yarn in Front

GLOSSARY

SPECIAL TECHNIQUES

BINDING OFF OVER CABLED FABRICS

To prevent edge flaring when binding off over cabling, bind off by working 2 stitches together out of every 4 stitches over cables. First, place a removable marker after the last stitch that is to be bound off, so that you do not lose count while decreasing and binding off at the same time. Then, work 1 stitch, *k2tog (or p2tog), pass previous stitch on R needle over stitch just worked, [work 1 stitch, pass previous stitch on R needle over stitch just worked] twice; repeat from * until the stitch you marked has been bound off.

ONE-ROW BUTTONHOLE

Step 1: With RS facing, work to buttonhole location. Bring yarn to the front of the work, slip the next stitch purlwise and bring the yarn to the back. *Slip another stitch and pass the previous slipped stitch over (1 stitch bound off); repeat from * until you have bound off the desired number of stitches (do not use working yarn to bind off).
Step 2: Slip the last stitch on the R needle back to the L needle and turn the work around (WS will be facing you). Insert the R needle between the first and second stitches on the L needle.

Wrap yarn around as if to knit and draw up a new loop, place this loop onto the L needle (1 stitch cast on). Continue to cast on stitches in this manner until you have cast on the number of stitches that were bound off + 1 additional stitch.
Step 3: Turn the work again (RS now facing). Slip the first stitch from the L needle to the R needle and pass the extra cast-on stitch over. Slip the last stitch on the R needle back to the L needle and continue as established.

SHORT ROWS: TURN & SLIP METHOD

Turn & slip:

On a RS or WS row: Work to specified point, turn work (opposite side facing now), slip 1 stitch purlwise, clip a locking marker or coilless safety pin around the working yarn, now prepare to work back in the opposite direction. There will be a gap between the slipped stitch and the stitch next to it.

On the following row, you will work to the gap and close it as follows:

If the first stitch after the gap is a knit stitch: Gently pull on the locking marker and place the loop of yarn onto the L needle (making sure right leg of loop is in front), then knit the next stitch together with the loop, removing the marker or coilless safety pin.

If the first stitch after the gap is a purl stitch: Slip next stitch on L needle to R needle, gently pull on the removable marker and place the loop of yarn onto the L needle (making sure right leg of loop is in front), return the stitch that you just slipped to the L needle, then purl the loop together with that stitch, removing marker or coilless safety pin.

SLOPED BIND OFF

Step 1: Work the first bind off rows at the garment edges as usual.
Step 2: One row before the next bind off row, work to the last stitch of the row, turn.

Step 3: Slip the first stitch from the L needle purlwise, pass the unworked stitch of the previous row over the slipped stitch (the first stitch is bound off). Bind off the remaining stitches as usual.

STEAM BLOCKING

Lay finished project flat on an appropriate blocking surface, smoothing fabric flat with your hands. Pin garment or item to instructed dimensions (see *Schematic*), using T-pins if necessary. Set your iron to the wool setting (medium temperature with steam) and prepare a press cloth (a flat cotton or linen tea towel or piece of cloth of similar weight) by soaking it in water and wringing it out. Lay the damp cloth over the knitted piece and hold the iron about ½" above the cloth, sending bursts of steam through the cloth. The damp cloth will add extra steam and prevent you from accidentally scorching the piece. Re-wet the cloth as needed. Move the cloth and steam each section of the knitting. Allow to dry completely before unpinning.

WET BLOCKING

Fill a sink or basin with warm water and a small amount of delicate dish soap or rinseless wool wash. Submerge fabric in water, gently squeezing out any air bubbles so that the piece can remain under water without being held there. Soak work for 30 minutes, allowing fabric to become completely saturated.

Drain the sink and remove work. If you have used dish soap (rather than rinseless wool wash), you will want to fill the sink again once or twice to rinse the soap from your fabric. Never place knitting directly under running water.

Squeeze out excess water from your work, taking care not to twist or wring fabric. Roll your fabric between two clean bath towels "burrito style" and firmly press towel roll. This will aid in removing moisture from the knitted piece. Remove piece from towels – your fabric should now feel damp but not saturated.

If blocking a flat project with blocking wires or a circular hat, proceed to the following instructions. Otherwise, lay fabric flat on a blocking board or other appropriate surface, gently coaxing project to schematic dimensions to air dry.

Blocking Wire Method (used for flat projects with long, straight edges):
Thread blocking wires along each edge of knitted piece at regular intervals. Along side edges, you will thread blocking wires using the running threads between your selvedge stitch and its inside neighboring stitch. Thread the blocking wires through the running thread every other row for a clean, even edge. Along bind-off edges, thread the blocking wires through the right leg of every stitch in the penultimate row (this is the last row of knitting before the bind off). Along cast-on edges, thread the blocking wires through the right leg of every stitch in the first row of knitting (this is the row you worked directly into your cast on).

Pin blocking wires in place on a blocking board or other appropriate surface, using instructed dimensions. If using T-pins only, use as many pins as required to block piece into desired shape. Allow fabric to air dry completely before removing.

Flat Method for Circular Hat:
Lay finished project flat on an appropriate blocking surface, smoothing fabric flat with your hands and allowing crown to naturally curve upward. Take care to not stretch the ribbed brim during blocking.

INFO

CREDITS

BOOK

JARED FLOOD
Editor & Creative Director

SARAH POPE
Copywriter

ANNA MOORE
Graphic Layout

JENNY TRYGG
Book Design

PATTERNS

MICHELE WANG
Knitwear Designer

ROBIN MELANSON
Senior Technical Editor

SUE MCCAIN
Technical Editor

JEN HURLEY
Proofreader

CHRISTINA RONDEPIERRE
Proofreader

PHOTOGRAPHY

JARED FLOOD
Photographer

ELIZABETH MCMURTRY
Wardrobe Stylist

JESSICA BELKNAP
Hair & Make Up

MONICA WATSON
Model

HARRY BAECHTEL
Model

LOCATION
Portland, Oregon
#TheAptUpstairs

KEEP IN TOUCH

Instagram: @brooklyntweed
Twitter: @brooklyntweed
Email: info@brooklyntweed.com

ORDERING INFORMATION

Interested in stocking this book in your bookstore or
yarn shop? Wholesale inquiries may be submitted
via email to the address below.

Published by Brooklyn Tweed
www.brooklyntweed.com
wholesale@brooklyntweed.com

PRINTED IN THE USA

This book is printed on Forest Stewardship Council®
certified paper. FSC® certification ensures that the
paper in this publication contains fiber from well
managed and responsibly harvested forests that meet
strict environmental and socioeconomic standards.

ISBN: 978-0-9976273-1-2

First Edition
January 2017